Children for Adoption

Books by Pearl S. Buck

Nonfiction

64 Children for Adoption [handwritten]

Friend to Friend
  (with Carlos P. Romulo)
'54. My Several Worlds
'50 The Child Who Never Grew
American Argument
Talk about Russia
What America Means to Me
'61 A Bridge for Passing

Of Men and Women
How It Happens
Tell the People
American Unity and Asia
Fighting Angel *57*
The Exile *36*
The Chinese Novel
  (Nobel Prize Lecture)

Fiction

[handwritten left margin]
The New Year 68
The Time Is Noon 67
The Three Daughters of Madame Liang 69
The Rainbow 74
MANDALA '70
DEATH IN THE CASTLE 65
SATAN NEVER SLEEPS 62
ALL UNDER HEAVEN '73
HEARTS COME HOME '71
The Story Bible I & II 71
The Goddess Abides 72
The Complete Woman 71
Once Upon A Xmas '50

The Living Reed *63*
Fourteen Stories *43*
Command the Morning *59*
Letter from Peking *51*
Come, My Beloved *53*
Imperial Woman *56*
The Hidden Flower *52*
God's Men *51*
Pavilion of Women *46*
Kinfolk *49*
Peony *48*
Portrait of a Marriage *45*
Voices in the House *53*
Bright Procession
The Angry Wife *47*
Far and Near *34*
The Promise *42*

Dragon Seed *41*
Today and Forever *34*
Other Gods *38*
The Patriot *39*
This Proud Heart *38*
A House Divided *35* (III)
The Mother *34*
The First Wife and Other
  Stories *33*
Sons *32* (II)
The Good Earth *31* (I)
East Wind: West Wind *30*
The Townsman *45*
The Long Love *49*
All Men Are Brothers
  (Shui Hu Chuan) *'33*
    translated from the Chinese *37*

Juveniles

Christmas Miniature *'52*
My Several Worlds
  (abridged for younger
  readers)
54 The Beech Tree
54 Johnny Jack and His
  Beginnings
'52 One Bright Day

The Big Wave *47*
The Man Who Changed China *'53*
Yu Lan: Flying Boy of China *45*
The Dragon Fish *44*
The Water-Buffalo Children *43*
The Chinese Children Next Door *42*
Stories for Little Children *40*
The Christmas Ghost ?
  (ONCE UPON A CHRISTMAS)
    Book '50

❉

CHILDREN
for
ADOPTION

———

Pearl S. Buck

❉

RANDOM HOUSE   NEW YORK

❀

THIS BOOK IS DEDICATED

TO

The Adopted

Oh! Why does the wind blow upon me so wild?
Is it because I am nobody's child?

—PHILA HENRIETTA CASE

Contents

Contents

Children for Adoption

I

Who Are the Orphans?

When I close my eyes and look back over my life I
see children, thousands of children, crowding in from
every part of the world where I have ever been; children of all ages and sizes; babies crying because they
are born; wistful toddlers; runabout children losing
their teeth; belligerent, hostile, eager teen-agers; children of every nation and race—children I know.

Where do they come from? Chinese children,
flocking around me when I was a child myself—these
are the first. I had no American children to play with
and all the children then were Chinese. Some of them

were children of my parents' friends, but most of them were just children. When we stopped at a village inn to rest for an hour on some journey, children seemed to spring out of the Chinese earth. They were there, dozens of them, hundreds of them, a surrounding sea of bright, interested faces, not too clean, many runny noses, much tousled sunburned dark hair, lively dark eyes and, if we stayed long enough, small hands reaching out to touch the stuff of our garments or to clasp our hands.

How well I remember the touch of those small hands! The Chinese have beautiful hands, and the hands even of the village children, unkempt and dirty, were finely shaped. And if we stopped to shop in a city street, then the street outside was crowded with children as far as sight could reach. The shop was open on one side, and unless the shopkeeper frowned and shouted—which he did, but mildly, for in Asia all children are a national treasure—the shop would have been filled with children, too.

"Why are you staring?" the shopkeeper invariably demanded of the children. "These honorable foreigners are human beings like ourselves."

At this the children always laughed, their eyes bright with doubt, and the shopkeeper laughed, and finally so did we. A child in China is—or was—a privileged citizen. I do not know what he is nowadays, under Communism, but in the days when I was a child the family in China was still the chief unit in society and children were its concern, first to get them born and then to love and nurture them into wise, competent human beings, always to be a credit to the family. We had no police and needed none, because the family was responsible for all its members. I knew one household where there was what we would call a delinquent, a son who grew into a wilfull, irresponsible man, bringing constant shame upon the family in spite of long patience and continuing love. At last the father and head of that family realized that matters could no longer continue as they were. One day he called the incorrigible son into the ancestral hall, and after explaining to him why there must be final punishment, he took a pistol from the table drawer and shot the young man dead. All had agreed to this as necessity, but the family went into deep and inconsolable mourning for the dead young man nevertheless. From the Western point of view, it was a shocking decision. From the family-founded Asian point of view, it was an act of the highest honor and a proof of respect for family and society. The child in Asia is loved not only for its own sake but as a symbol of hope for the future of both family and nation.

Love—that is what I think of when I see in my memory those Asian child faces. They were children who were loved, rich or poor. I renewed the memory on a recent long visit to India. There the children were again, hundreds upon thousands. Our work took us into villages and cities, and wherever we went the same bright eyes were intent upon our every movement, the great beautiful eyes of India's children, dark under lashes so long and curly that any Hollywood star might feel envy without hope of emulation. So many children there were that one might have thought them homeless and uncared for. Yet every child had the look of a wanted child, and if one child cried because of being pushed or falling, a mother, elder sister or brother appeared instantly for the rescue. Seemingly on their own, the children of India are under the constant, watchful eyes of love. Thin from hunger, they have whatever anyone has, and the elders go hungrier than they. All but naked in the hot Indian sun, they appear in bright garb upon a holiday. Burdened under brass pots of water as they walk in single file from the well to the home, they run as free as rabbits when work is done. Oh, those beautiful children! I leaned from the window of my hotel at dawn and saw them in the long line of water-carrying, their slender bodies, naked except for a loin cloth, dark against the rosy sky, a frieze of living grace.

And when I traveled northward to the foot of the Himalayas I saw other children, the precious children of Tibetan refugees. They had crossed the perilous mountains on foot with their elders, they had come through passes all but impassable, over ice and snow, along precipitous, winding footpaths. The little ones, the babies and the toddlers, I am sure were carried on the backs of men and women, but the rest, the three- and four-year-olds and upward, walked. When their shoes had worn away, their feet were bound in rags and they continued to walk.

"They are our treasure, our hope for survival as a people," the young Dalai Lama told me when I visited him in India.

"Would you like me to find some adoptive families for them in the United States?" I asked. "It would not be hard—they are handsome children and very intelligent."

He shook his head. "We cannot spare one—not one. The Communists have taken thousands of our children to China, and those we have lost. These are the ones we have saved. We will do our best for them."

They *were* doing their best for them. I saw in every Tibetan refugee center that the children were the heart and the reason for living. The best food, the best shelter, were given to them, and the elders, whether parents or not, and the lamas were doing their utmost to give them not only food and housing but education in the Tibetan culture and in the culture, too, of India —India, who gives them shelter while they are homeless.

Love of children manifests itself everywhere throughout Asia. The children of Japan go to school, in Tokyo or in the remotest seashore villages, all nicely dressed in Western clothes, all carrying knapsacks of books and small thermos bottles, all clean and scrubbed, hair brushed, neat shoes and socks, treasured children, boys and girls alike. And in the Philippine Islands there are the same children, the dearly loved. Even Hong Kong, the most crowded and congested area in the world and stretched beyond all capacity by the influx of refugees from Communist China, somehow manages to keep its children clean and bright. They tramp in over the border weary and hungry and often in tears, but in a miraculously few days they are consoled, washed and fed.

Why do I tell of the children of Asia, when this book is about American children? For this reason: in a peculiar, unprecedented, unparalleled way, the children of Asia are loved as ours are not. Yes, of course we love our children, but somehow it is not with the same respectful, accepting love, a love which, while it disciplines and controls, yet recognizes the divine in the human being, and the individual's right to be himself. In the family-oriented society of Asia—again I am not speaking of Communist China—the child had, and has, a special place. I did see an occasional child—especially girls—who, sold as a slave or bondmaid in time of catastrophe, oftentimes to save her life lest she starve with her elders in a famine, might be ill-treated if her mistress was cruel. But she would be the exception, although it is true that boy children were treated better on the whole than girl children. Yet the unusual does not deny the usual, and usually children were treated with love, even though they must share the sufferings and deprivations of their elders.

Will this continue as Asia moves into industrial development? It may not. Inevitably the individual becomes less important in an industrial society. The big protecting family tends to break up into the small unit of individual parents and their children, and the wisdom and kindliness of older people are lost. It will take time, nevertheless, for Asian tradition and habit to pass, if pass it must. Meanwhile I make the point that in Asia I never saw what I see in my own country, the many children who are orphans in fact and in effect, children born out of wedlock and therefore dependent upon adoption for families, although most of them are never adopted; children growing up in orphanages; babies staying in the hospitals where they were born because there is nowhere for them to go. I confess that the sight of these children shocks and grieves me.

Who are these orphaned children? Years ago I asked the question and I am still asking it. They are children of many races, but all born in the United States except for the children fathered by American men on military duty in Asian countries. And strangest of all to me, reared as I was in Asia where there is total freedom of religion, there are children in my own country who are born Catholic, Protestant, Lutheran or Presbyterian, this or that, and who remain orphans because of religion. For in addition to race there are also here the barriers of religion, so that in actuality children are orphaned by the hold of the organization upon the unborn.

Where do they come from, these children? Statistics say that some two hundred and fifty thousand children are born out of wedlock in the United States every year, and the number is rising. A quarter of a million unwanted children born every year in the United States of America! This does not take into account other unwanted children—orphans whose parents are dead or divorced, or who cannot or will not care for them for personal or economic reasons. The total is unreported, so far as I can find. I know of no such situation in any other country and I set myself to discover, in a search that covers twenty years in time, why there are so many unwanted children in my own country, and what, if anything, can be done about it.

Monogamy is partly responsible. In China there would also have been illegitimate children, as they are called here, if it had not been the rule to take into the family any woman who was pregnant but not married. A man was held responsible for his own seed, and his children, too precious to be wasted as orphans or homeless waifs, were brought into his family. The mother became his concubine. She was not a wife and she displaced no one. She was a woman who had her place in the house, and her children were recognized equally with the children of the real wife, whom they called mother, while the concubine who was their mother they called aunt. In short, all the children a man begot belonged to him and to his wife. From the child's point of view, there were many advantages in this system, but I realize that it is impractical in our culture, euphemistically called monogamous. That there are some quarter of a million children born out of wedlock every year means that our society should be recognized as polygamous in effect if not in name.

The real tragedy of our children, I repeat, is that so many of them are not wanted. These quarter of a million children born in the United States every year are not wanted, or they would not be given for adoption. Or put it this way: the woman's natural instinct to keep and care for her young is not strong enough to stand against our society's condemnation and punishment for bearing a child out of wedlock, a child called "illegitimate." The father of such a child assumes no responsibility and our society makes no demands upon him. The woman may give her child away and then go free, too, except for her personal sense of guilt, if she has any. It is the child who bears alone the total burden of his illegitimate birth. His best hope is adoption, but there are countless children who are not allowed adoption, and who therefore will never realize their full development because they are kept in orphanages and foster homes, for one reason or another. It is bad for a child to know that his family, perhaps the only one he will ever have, is no more than a foster family, one who cannot or will not give him a legal family name and an assured place in society. He may be grateful for whatever love and kindness he gets from them but in his heart of hearts, as he grows older, he knows that he does not belong and that they are paid to care for him. It takes a great deal of love to overcome the fact that the people who stand as his parents in practical terms get paid for doing so. It means he is never quite sure of them.

Even the unmarried mother is not so fortunate here as, for example, she is in Sweden. There the public accepts this lone mother. She even has the right to call herself Mrs. instead of Miss. When a Swedish woman, not married, knows she is pregnant, she may apply for help from the state, and if necessary, she may live in housing supported by the state, although she does not, usually, remain in a state-supported home for more than a year. By that time she is adjusted to her life with the child and she is given the same respect as other women who have not had her experience. She is encouraged to return to work after the child is born, she is encouraged to keep her child and to live, as far as possible, a normal life. The American woman, when she is an unmarried mother, simply disappears for a while from her community and then comes back, childless, her secret hidden for life.

II

Sex and Unwanted Children

Who is this unmarried mother in American society? She is anyone. Most often she comes from the middle class but that, perhaps, is merely because most people belong to that class. She comes, too, from the extremes —from the poor and deprived, and from the high level of wealth and culture. There is no telling who she is but she is legion. There were more than fourteen thousand children of unwed mothers born last year in New York City alone. Of these, more than a thousand were born to girls under seventeen years of age. Many if not most of these girls left their homes and families out of fear and went to live in some agency shelter for unwed mothers. Of course these young girls were frightened. They knew they were too young and they feared death in childbirth, but more than death they feared what their mothers and fathers would say, especially their mothers. Mothers of young unwed mothers have something to do with all this, if we are to believe what psychiatrists tell us. The girl who becomes an unwed mother, we are told, is sick and already emotionally disturbed. This disturbance, we are to believe, comes from a disturbed family life. What was wrong with the family life? Many things, it seems. This girl, this unwed young mother, has felt herself rejected by her mother or her father, but especially by her mother, and she retaliates by a primitive act of procreation. She may be lonely in her family group and therefore emotionally starved, or she may have a fantasy of incestuous relationship with her father and of having a baby by him. She may have a sense of guilt because she has broken childhood rules and done so secretly. Often, and perhaps most likely, she simply has an upsurge of physical desire, which she has not yet learned to discipline.

Yet how can we consider the unwed mother apart from our present stage in society? Her problem, if she has a problem, may only be that she is living in this era of phenomenal change in our national life. No people in the world has changed as much as the American since the end of the Second World War, with the exception of Communist China. We have grown in many ways, and it is too soon to tell whether the change is for the better or for the worse. Our new awareness of the world of nations and people, our amazing readiness to change as we come to know these other cultures, have shaken our society to its foundations and signify a restraining shell to our own culture, which has long been repressing inner expansion and the impulse for change.

Nowhere is this more apparent than in our new ethics of sex. Today's standards of sex morality, in practice and in theory, have changed radically, and this within little more than one generation in span of time. It is no wonder that there is widespread bewilderment and confusion. The change is so abrupt, so far-reaching, that we are all dazed by it. Nor can we comfort ourselves by saying that it is only the young who have changed. The new sex standards are to be found among men and women of any age, but especially among women. I specify, for the most significant change is in women. Even older women are allowing themselves a sexual freedom which would have horrified not only their mothers but themselves in the prewar period. They are still horrified enough to keep their secrets to themselves, and yet, half laughing, half shame-faced, they will confess to some woman friend that they are having extramarital affairs. Among unmarried women there is little shame, but still not much talk. I confess to my own sense of shock when a friend, an older unmarried woman, apparently of the highest respectability and with considerable public responsibility, told me tranquilly that she had only some time before carried on a two-year affair with an equally respectable but married man. She explained, with no sense of guilt, that she wanted to know what sexual experience was before she grew too old.

"Did you love the man?" I asked.

"No, but I liked him enough," she replied with calm.

"And why did you stop the affair?" I asked.

"His job was moved to another city and it was too inconvenient for us to meet," she said.

"Have you ever regretted it?" I asked.

"Not at all," she said. "I am very grateful to him and I think he is to me."

"But he was married," I argued. "Had you no concern for his wife?"

"He needed something more, and I supplied that need," she said. "I doubt he's had another affair. I rather imagine he's gone back to his wife and is quite contented. Indeed, he never left her, nor does she know, I am sure, because she was my friend, too—still is. We often have lunch together."

"And she really does not know?"

"Does not and never will."

And what about my handsome fifty-five-year-old friend, a divorcee, who, contemplating marriage with a man of her own age, felt that she could not proceed unless she knew what he would be as a sexual partner? He was satisfactory, but later she decided against him because they were unequal intellectually and perhaps socially. The common sense with which she came to this conclusion repudiated any feelings of guilt or loss of self-respect, and can only prove my point that our sex standards have changed, especially for women.

And yet, in one way I do not think the change in women is any greater than that in men, for men accept the change in women with surprising equanimity and even with pleasure. A generation ago they demanded virginity in their brides and chastity in their wives. Now half of the young women who marry, if I am to trust statistics, are not virgins. It does not seem to matter to most men whether they marry virgins or not. This can only mean a real equalization of sex standards, since women, always realistic where men are concerned, have neither required nor expected their husbands to be virgin at marriage. Hopefully, husbands would remain faithful after marriage, but women have always distrusted other women, and are watchful on this score, and ready to forgive the man at least once if the worst, though expected and feared, does happen.

I am reminded at this point of a recent conversation I had with a famous aging male film star in India. It was evening in the lovely little town of Limbdi, a hot golden evening, the stars blazing around a sliver of a new moon. We had been working all day in the desert and were relaxing on the upper terrace of what was euphemistically called the Maharajah's Guest House, but which was actually the house where his concubines had lived. There are very few maharajahs and concubines in this new age in India and the house had been standing empty until it was used by our cast and crew on a motion picture project. There we were, then, on the upper terrace, sitting in peace as our Indian friends drank prohibition liquor. Our famous star had been expounding on his favorite subject, women.

"Do Indian men still expect their wives to be faithful to them?" I asked, half idly. The answer was so fiercely in the affirmative that I quickly asked the next question: "Do Indian women expect their husbands to be faithful?"

Silence followed this. Then the handsome old actor cleared his throat, took a swallow of whiskey, and replied in his best manner.

"Let me answer from my own experience, Madame! After all, what man do I know so well as myself? When I am—ah, attracted to a young woman for whatever reason, I regret it very much. Nevertheless it happens. I am sad. Yet it happens. I try not to let my wife know how I suffer. But she is a wise woman. And she knows me after all these years of marriage. She observes my suffering. Does she reprove me? No! She is silent for a time. At last she speaks. And what does she say? She comes to me humbly. 'Darling,' she says, 'how have I failed you?' And I say, in my misery, 'Shut up! Don't say anything.'

"So she, always obedient, says nothing. She waits. In due course the affair ends. Now I go to her. 'Forgive me,' I say. 'Take me back. I am here.' And she says, 'Darling, I love you. I have always loved you.'"

A profound silence follows this disclosure. I break the silence with a final question.

"And you, do you love your wife?"

A silence still more profound follows this question.

The old actor, under the influence of liquor, is struggling to find the truth. He speaks at last, his magnificent voice at its best.

"I," he says, and the pronoun rolls out upon the evening air, "I—respect her!"

There is nothing more to be said. We change the subject. And he continues to live in a generation that is passing in India, as it is passing, perhaps has passed, in the United States.

"Another ten years," a young Indian tells me the next day, "and our women will be like yours, they will demand equal opportunity for sin."

"Only it will not be considered or called sin," I reply, remembering how short a time ago it was called sin in my own country, but now no more.

Our women? What will they be ten years from now? They will be the women who emerge from the many girls at school and college today. And who and what are these girls? They are any girls, girls from all walks of life, poor girls and rich girls. They are amazingly pretty, most of them, and some of them are even beautiful. With every cosmetic aid acceptable, with none of the old handicaps of prejudice against paint and powder, hair dye and figure-shaping garments, the result is almost uniformly pleasing to the eye. They are not stupid, these girls, but neither are they industrious. Many of them will be unwed mothers, sooner or later, and most of them, or more and more of them, are already potential unwed mothers. That is to say, if we are to trust statistics, not only are half of them not virgins on their wedding day, but if we are to believe the reports from the *Journal of the National Association of Women Deans and Counselors*, about one-fourth of the undergraduate students at college are already having sex relations with men and the number is increasing all the time. Chastity until engagement is the ultimate present-day goal for young women, it seems.

Of course secrecy, I repeat, is still maintained. Enough of the past remains for that. We Americans are loath to give up our dreams. We know, but we will not believe, that our young people are not more pure than other young people. Girl students are still expelled from college and from high schools when they become pregnant. Pregnancy is the sin; the surface must be and is still being preserved. Parents cannot be told the truth. Truth is too much for the elders, the young people believe. Nevertheless the young tell more than they are aware of telling. The recent outburst of novels about undergraduate life and the sex standards thereof are very revealing in what their characters discuss and in what they do. Talk and action can be summed up in one word—*sex*. The mystery of it is that there is so little real sex in all this sex. The sex act is here an isolated experience, separate from the world and its rich life. And sex expressed only in the sex act is not enough sex for anyone.

It is not enough even in these new novels about the young. The sex act repeated again and again becomes as dull as any other routine, and the characters who perform it have neither variety nor charm. A dreadful indifference sets in. The two concerned are as unconcerned, while they go about their routine, as though the sex act were expected of them as a duty and they get on with it as quickly as possible, a physical performance. For example, in a recent television series, presented as a public service, the following conversation took place between a girl, the boy who had made the young girl pregnant, and a reporter.

REPORTER: Most of the guys from our way of living —from our stick of life—they go with a girl, and sex to them is just like eating rice and beans and—

BOY: Yeah.

REPORTER: —and it's something—you know, man, it's there, you grab it and forget it. Right?

BOY: Hm, hmm.

(23)

REPORTER: How come you didn't just grab it and forget it?

BOY: Because I went for this girl and I still go for her.

REPORTER: How strong do you go?

GIRL: All the way.

REPORTER: Do you know any of these girls that— they got a baby but they ain't got no guy that stood by them?

GIRL: Well, sometimes they just—you know, they have a baby from one guy; they just, you know, be working for at least two or three weeks, and then they follow another guy, and they start goin' with this guy, and they have another baby from this guy. They just keep on—you know—havin' babies from other guys.

Obviously this girl comes from a group limited by family environment and lack of education, but the same casual attitude toward sex is to be found among girls of higher cultural background, where it seems the standard increasingly is that sex is permissible wherever there is affection or attraction. Taking these two levels and finding the norm somewhere between them, it is apparent that the actual and the permissible have no relation to responsibility either to family or to the unborn child. It depends entirely upon personal feeling, however temporary, without regard for consequences, even for the individual herself or himself.

"We don't have to be ashamed," a young man summed it up. "We only pretend we are, anyway, to be polite."*

Shame put aside, let us examine the cause and effect of this atmosphere in which we live, an atmosphere sulphurous with physical sex. Sex has become a commercial commodity. Sex sells, the merchants have discovered. Advertising is sugar-coated with sex, and theater is based overwhelmingly on sex. Producers, as I can testify from my own experience, weigh a play by the amount of sex and violence in it, but especially sex, for violence is now reaching a surfeit point with the public, while sex is not.

"Fifty percent sex, fifty percent violence is O.K. in a play," a producer advised me, "but seventy percent sex and thirty percent violence is better. Of course for some audiences you can reverse the figures and still get by."

Now, I myself have no prejudice against sex, and so declared some time ago in a lecture room at Columbia University. There was a question period after the lecture, and the most eager question was the one that a young woman had just put to me.

* See *Mademoiselle,* August, 1963, article entitled "Lady Chatterley Goes to College," by Nancy Lynch.

"What have you to say about the preponderant sex interest in the new novels?" she asked. "We had a novelist here the other day lecturing to us, who thought there was too much sex in these novels. Do you agree with him?"

I considered for a moment and then made my attempt to answer out of my own life, which has been rich in varied relationships with men.

"There is no doubt," I said, "that sex is the most important thing in life. But when I say sex I mean everything that goes on or can go on between men and women, of which the physical sex act is only a part, although sometimes a culminating, fulfilling part. When I say sex I mean all the give-and-take in ordinary life between men and women in business, in passing, in casual delightful friendships, in deep absorbing friendships that never become physical, although they might so become at a particular moment, which may arrive or may not. Sex is everywhere, it ought to be everywhere, it does and should permeate the life of men and women as long as they live, for without each other, men and women are sorry half-creatures. That is why I deplore the fact that women are not in the policy-making places of our nation, for there sex is lacking, and it ought not to be, and unbalance is the result. Men and women must live together, work together, achieve together on every level of constructive creative life of mind and spirit, national and international, if there is to be peace and harmony in the world. Occasionally they will meet intimately, but I believe that marriage is the best place for this meeting, for I have always in mind the child that may result from such a meeting. A child needs father and mother all its life, if possible, and certainly until maturity. So when you ask if I think there is too much sex in the new novels I answer by saying no, there is too little —too little and too limited, for in those books sex is too often merely physical, and when the physical precedes all the wonderful whole of sex, it loses its meaning. It becomes an elimination rather than a source of new power and creative strength. I am all for more and better sex, a more complete communication between men and women, which, while it should and must include the physical act of love upon suitable occasion, would place the physical in its proper and most satisfying relation to the whole."

Unfortunately our present limited understanding of sex has not only produced an enormous crop of orphaned children every year, but has also spread its damage to other countries, where even our inadequate methods of birth control are not known or cannot be used because of their relatively high cost and techniques too difficult for unsophisticated societies. Our American men, stationed as soldiers or other personnel in the Asian countries of Japan, Korea, Vietnam, Okinawa and elsewhere, have left behind them thousands of half-American children, who can find no place in the cultures of the countries where they are born. It is difficult for Americans to realize how a half-white or half-Negro child stands out among a people all of one color and with one type of hair. These little ones, who look Oriental when they are brought to the United States, look American in the countries where they were born. I am sensitive to this, for I grew up as a white American child among Chinese people, and though they were kindly they were curious, and their comments on my hair and eyes, which were unfavorable, and on the whiteness of my skin, left me with a feeling of difference and isolation. I can therefore understand the sensitivity of our own Negroes in a country predominantly white. In my case there was no damage, for I had my American family and ample security. Moreover, the Chinese were friendly and accepting, after the initial surprise at my strange appearance.

Not so for the little half-American children now

growing up in Asian countries, and for those who will continue to be born there, since our men are stationed widely. The children do not, I hope and believe, meet with actual cruelty, but they have no security whatsoever. Their mothers have gone beyond the pale in bearing them to white men, who cannot offer them the legal status of concubine, and therefore in many cases, perhaps in most, these women are outcasts. Moreover, comparatively few of the American men stand by the Asian women whom they have impregnated. Perhaps they do not even know that their relationship, usually brief, has resulted in a child. The half-American children are orphans, therefore, and have no outlook for the future in countries where a family is still necessary if a child is to get an education and find a job later. They are growing up, these orphans, as outcasts. In some countries, as in Korea, a girl who has a child out of wedlock has no recourse, when the man responsible has gone, except to become a prostitute. The half-American child then is doomed to share this life with the mother.

True, a limited number of agencies are bringing some of these children to the United States for adoption. The policy of our own military officials, however, is that they can make no recognition of the existence of children fathered by Americans, and therefore that they must belong to the countries where they were born. This seems to me a singularly unrealistic attitude; first, because our men are responsible for these children, who would never have been born otherwise, and second, because these countries cannot handle such children and have no means of providing for them within their social structure, at least in time to save this generation. Nor is adoption in the United States anything but a partial solution for a limited number. Our immigration regulations are so severe that only the best—the healthiest and most intelligent —can enter the land of their fathers. This means that the ones left behind are inferior and will remain as a permanent stigma for the United States. "Look what the Americans left us!" is what the Asians are saying.

I confess that as an American I find it embarrassing, to say the least, when I see upon the street of a Korean town a child in rags and filth who, putting out a scrawny hand to beg, lifts to me eyes of American blue, peering from beneath hair tangled and dirty and lice-ridden, but red or blond. I do not say that Koreans are unkind to these children, and usually their prostitute mothers love them. But they have no place and no future. Our young men ought never to have fathered them. Do not, I beg, ask me how it might have been prevented. I do not know, since sex is as free as the air in our country, albeit not as pure. I simply say that these children should never have been born, any more than the two hundred and fifty thousand in our own country should have been born. But since they were born, and since such children will continue to be born until and unless we think of them as human beings and devise a society in which they can live among us as human beings, they are displaced persons, born displaced, because there is no place for them anywhere. They are a new breed, without family, without country. Yet it is we who have created them. We have a responsibility, however much we may deny or neglect it.

What of the mothers of these world's children? How did it come about that they capitulated so quickly and easily to our American men, those Asian women, who have lived so closely guarded, so strictly restrained, so accustomed to freedom for men and not for women? Family in Asia as everywhere in the world is founded upon paternalism, the insistence of man that he know that his woman's child comes of his own seed. Anthropologically, in the early days of human beings upon this earth, woman, though accessible to man, lived with her child. It was not even known that man was partly responsible for the child, and man and woman alike believed that woman produced the child spontaneously and alone, the inspiration coming perhaps from the divine power of the sun, this power brought to earth by the flying birds. Hence the legend of the stork bringing the baby, hence the legend of angels, hence the legend even of the Holy Spirit descending in the form of a dove. But some early scientist, undoubtedly male, put two and two together and recognized the fact that within a certain space of time following intercourse a child was born. Woman was then dethroned, not only in the eyes of the suddenly important and essential male, but also in her own eyes, as it became obvious that she could not produce a child entirely alone, a dethronement from which, I fear, she has not yet fully recovered. As for man, he became inflated to the point of wanting to be sure of his paternity and therefore he sequestered his woman and denied her availability to any other man, and so the family was founded. In China, for example, man declared that small bound feet were beautiful, whereupon woman at once began to bind her feet. Woman will always do whatever man declares makes her beautiful, and women with bound feet could only hobble and therefore never wandered far. Yet the Asian is realistic, however flowery his language. Man and woman both understood that a man finds it difficult to limit his sexual activities to one woman. Polygamy was therefore allowed, although as I have said, all women who receive a man's seed must come under his roof so that his children would not be wasted.

A notable example of exception to this sequestration existed in Tibet, and a few other places, where a man offered his woman to a guest as a courtesy, or where several brothers shared one woman's bed. The reason for this was partly economic, since wives and marriage are expensive in Tibet, and children are very valuable. For example, a husband who was infertile could hope for a child by a guest or a brother, and for all practical purposes the child was his. In China, however, this sharing would have been unthinkable, as it would also have been in Japan. In pre-Communist China, early and arranged marriages made unwed mothers impossible. I never heard of one. Unfaithful wives were punished by death, and the practice thereby discouraged. In both countries, China and Japan, women were divided sharply into two classes: respectable wives, and women who entertained men. In Japan this distinction still holds, although the dividing line is not so clear as it was before the American Occupation.

If we have affected the Asian culture, however, through our charming males—and Asian women have found our men very charming indeed and there have

been many genuine love matings—Asian women also
have greatly affected our men. Since male acquaintance has been mostly with the female group that is
socially available to men, such as hostesses in night
clubs, geisha, actresses, and so on, relationships have
easily slipped into physical sex, especially because
communication by language is difficult and physical
sex is the same in any language, or without language.
Our young men, accustomed to parental strictures and
until the end of the war to the reluctance of the American women to enter into sexual entanglements, found
the Asian women acquiescent and delightful in their
easy submission. Sex in Asia has always been somewhat
apart from love, as evidenced in most of the love
poetry, where, unless the man and woman are married,
the lover sighs because his beloved is inaccessible and
cannot be reached at all or only through few and brief
meetings. Those women whom the American men met
in Asia, therefore, were usually the available sort, for
whom sex meant business primarily, but they had been
trained in the art of sex, which to the American man,
unaccustomed to such skills, meant love. There was
a great deal of heartbreak on both sides if love did
enter into the situation and if marriage was impossible.
Even where there was marriage, love too often proved
insufficient to weather the differences. I do not know

of any study made of these marriages, and therefore I have no means of knowing how successful they have been between American men and Asian women in statistical terms. I can only judge by the number of children from such marriages who have been given for adoption, as well as the number I have seen in the streets of Asia.

Let me return to the question of why many Asian women yield to American men in sex without marriage. While it is true that the majority who yield to our men are entertainers or prostitutes, there are others, and I am inclined to believe that their submission is due to two reasons: first, Asian women are, generally speaking, emotionally starved, and second, those who yield are not only the weaker ones but without hope for themselves because they are women. Asian behavior patterns provide little emotional outlet for girls and women. Indian men, for example, complain privately of the passivity of their wives. Actually Indian women are far from passive in other aspects of life, and if they are passive in love it is because the circumstances of their lives have restricted their emotional development. A lusty young Englishman in Bombay recently put it thus: "These Indian girls look beautiful and romantic but they are lousy lovers." Perhaps so, yet when an Indian woman does wake up and fall in love, she is

ready to leave home and children and follow her beloved to any country with amazing abandon.

One reason for the seeming passivity or detachment
of the Asian women may be the early separation between men and women. This custom still prevails to
some extent, although modern life is changing it slowly
through coeducational schools and through women's
increasing participation in industry. Yet in the family
there is a separation, and if not the actual separation,
which removes the boy from the women's quarters at
the age of seven, there is nevertheless a real difference
in the treatment of son and daughter. The boy is always
more welcome from birth on, and the girl knows this.
Special advantages are given him, special privileges
are his. The girl learns early to subdue her own feelings
and to yield to the male. She seldom hears the words of
love. Even in marriage love may never be spoken,
though it may exist. In Japan particularly, to speak of
an emotion was to degrade it. Love was to be expressed
by devoted acts rather than by words. Girls grew up
believing themselves inferior to their fathers and their
brothers, and therefore to their husbands. When
American men came with their easy love words, their
embraces and kisses, it is no wonder that the Asian
girls were dazed and overwhelmed.

Then, too, one must take into account the known

fact that when a conquering army enters a vanquished country the women psychologically feel the impulse to yield themselves in the total surrender. This is historically true, as is also the expectation, half-unconscious but real, that victorious soldiers accept the submission of women in the subjected country and feel that they deserve the release. Undoubtedly one of the enchantments of war, to my knowledge never yet fully analyzed, lies in the anticipated surrender of women to the conquering males. The enchantment exists for both man and woman in their respective rôles. I lived for most of my life in a warring era of China's modern history, in the midst of revolutionary struggle and military contests between competing leaders, and I observed this phenomenon repeatedly. There was both horror and excitement among the populace when an army approached, and when the battle was over, the ensuing rape of women was the grand finale, after which the curtain went down. Nor is this an Asian trait alone. The same situation prevailed in Germany after the war ended, and if the crop of babies was not so obvious as it was in Asian countries it was only because both parents were white. When the American father was Negro, exactly the same displacement occurred and the half-Negro child found neither welcome nor status in the land of his birth. The Germans were not accustomed to dark Germans, and the half-Negro children suffered much until some provision could be made for them, mainly in orphanages. It remains to be seen what will happen to them as they grow into adulthood. Germany does not have a good record of absorbing special peoples. Such information as I have, however, is of course only from West Germany.

In our country the thesis of a disturbed or inadequate emotional life seems to furnish the most reliable reason for premarital sex. Dr. Ner Littner, of the Department of Psychiatry at the Reese Hospital in Chicago, sets forth this theory with clarity in his article "The Natural Parents," one of the scientific papers presented in January, 1955, at the National Conference on Adoption. He suggests, in effect, that many girls feel unlovable because of a disturbed relationship with their mothers. When an emotional event occurs, such as a new relationship with a man which seems unlikely to result in marriage, an anxiety is added to an already anxious nature and the girl tries to achieve an emotional balance by becoming pregnant. It is also suggested that the mother has a subconscious wish to have another child; the daughter knows this and tries to please her mother by becoming pregnant, in a sense, for her. Sometimes the daughter gives her child to the mother; in other cases the social worker becomes the mother figure and the child is given to her.

My own observation of unwed mothers confirms the probability that they have long felt themselves unlovable. Most of them are not particularly attractive in appearance, especially the younger ones. There are, of course, notable exceptions, especially among those over eighteen. But the younger ones are too often pathetic, and one can well imagine that in their natural search for love they are willing to attract boys and men by any means in their power, and sex, alas, is all they have to give. Unhappily, it is usually the most welcome gift, and so a child is born.

One of the most interesting points in Dr. Littner's article is the brief section on the emotional control of ovulation. I have not seen, and cannot find, statistics on the percentage of pregnancies where there has been only one contact, but I can understand why unwed girls seem to become pregnant so much more easily than many married women, if what Dr. Littner says is true, as an "implied fact." The pregnancy, he says, is not an accident but occurs through some sort of emotional control over the unwed mother's ability to conceive. It is also interesting to note that while many of these unmarried mothers have the knowledge of contraceptives, which would make sexual intercourse safe, they "forgot" to use them. Again it is significant that such pregnancies seldom end in miscarriage. Unwed mothers reject abortions, nausea is rare, they feel well, they are serene, they produce fine healthy babies. The reason suggested for all this is that unwed mothers have created a condition that demands and gets them more attention from the mother and this provides a sort of reconciliation with her. Without following in detail these interesting ideas, one must agree with the conclusion that an unmarried mother's pregnancy is "an attempt at emotional recovery—of healing an emotional wound." Both in Asia and in our own country the theory of feeling unlovable and unwanted seems valid as a cause for a pregnancy which in most cases could have been avoided.

What of the unwed father? There is little information to be found about him. He seldom appears before the caseworker, and if he does, the interview is usually unsatisfactory, for he feels guilty and yet at the same time is afraid of marriage, and unwilling to accept responsibility. Since caseworkers are usually women, it may be that there is some unrecognized hostility here which prevents communication. Perhaps we should have male caseworkers handle the men. From my own experience with adoption, I can only conclude that these prospective fathers, whether young or not, also have feelings of deep inferiority. As much as the girls, they feel unlovable, and dreading the possibility of refusal if they propose marriage they choose the swifter, less responsible sex act. These young men, too, prefer not to use a contraceptive, for they have a definite wish to impregnate a girl as proof of masculinity and superiority. It is interesting to note that while our American men abroad were given contraceptives, or could get them free if they wished, relatively few men used them. It was also interesting to learn on a recent visit to India that while the Indian government provides free information about birth control and free contraceptives, men feel their virility incomplete, and therefore unsatisfactory, if they use contraceptives. Some men also prefer that women not use them. It seems apparent therefore that there is always the subconscious wish in both men and women for impregnation, and this, however much reason may demand that there be no child resulting from the connection.

In India, of course, children have the added value of being the only security against their parents' old age, and it is doubtful whether there can be much advance in birth control until some sort of social security is established through modern industry.

"With the child death rate so high as ours," an intelligent young Indian explained to me, "we cannot afford not to have children. Suppose my wife and I have ten children. In all likelihood five of them will die early. This leaves us only five children. Suppose three of them are girls. They will marry and go to other families. This leaves us only two sons. One of these may die by some accident even after he is grown. Can one remaining son care for his mother and me in our old age?"

Granted that this is a somewhat pessimistic view, it is possible that the man was right. In India, however, although one may be misled by the swarms of seemingly untended children pervading every nook and corner of the streets, the large family system still prevails, and will continue until industry develops to a degree comparable to its development in the West. Therefore the children all belong somewhere and to someone, and India does not yet face directly the problem of modern industrialization, which is the displaced child. The time is not too far off when increasing industrialization will come in India, too. Many Indians are aware of its effect upon the family, however, and are hoping somehow to retain the large family unit and keep it responsible for the child. It remains to be seen how this can be done. Industrialization came upon the United States swiftly and unawares, and we have not yet fully understood its social impact, in spite of many discussions and much research on the subject. Perhaps we know but shirk the knowledge that the responsibility of each community is to take care of its own, under the umbrella of state and federal concern and demand. It is much easier merely to place a neglected child in a detention home and forget about it than it is to provide for it in the community where the child has its family.

The query returns to our own country and the question of what to do with this large number of unwanted children by unmarried parents. The large family and its responsibility for each member, a situation essential to the agricultural society, seems impossible for the industrial society. There can be and there must be a solution, however. I believe it is to be found in some other organization that can and will take the place of the large family unit. This organization is the local community where the child is born. There must be a community responsibility if the small family unit is not strong enough to teach and care for the children it produces. State and federal agencies cannot be expected, and indeed are not able, to function on broad levels and at the same time to concern themselves with local and community needs. The warmth and friendliness of the home community is essential and it can and should assume responsibility for each member, as the small family unit takes the place of the old family group in an industrial society.

The problem in our present community life, however, is the lack of central organization which could co-ordinate the many agencies, both public and private, and thus prevent duplication and confusion, not to mention the draining of charitable funds. A community should have a council of respected and qualified citizens, made up of lay and professional persons under the leadership of the mayor, perhaps, and forming a group responsible for the welfare of all citizens, at least to the degree of knowing what services are available in the community and seeing to it that they are used by the citizens and for them. President Kennedy laid great stress on community responsibility in his effort to better the lot of the retarded child in our society. Where such local groups have been formed, as for example in some areas of Pennsylvania, they have worked admirably when leadership is competent.

Meanwhile we have the emotionally disturbed individuals, both male and female, who attempt to find in each other the comfort of a sex relationship. It is essential to find out why they exist. For the unmarried fathers show much the same neurotic tendencies that the unmarried mothers do, and I am inclined to think that by and large there are more such males than females in this area.

Too many American men are unstable emotionally, or at least undeveloped emotionally, generally speaking, and they do not understand sex although they crave it. They do not understand the subtleties, the delights, the finesse, of the relationship between men and women, and as a result they are inclined to oversimplify and to mistake the physical aspect for the whole. They emerge from the experience as unsatisfied as the woman and for exactly the same reason—they have not fully experienced sex at all, and discontent is inevitable. Lust is certainly a part of sex, but to quench lust alone and apart from the whole of sex is to quench one's thirst by drinking from a stale pond rather than from a living, flowing clear fountain.

The reason for this emotional immaturity comes, I believe, at least partly from the he-man image, the pioneer image so continually exemplified by what we call our "Westerns." The rough, tough individual, who gallops his way through the world, takes his women where he finds them and treats 'em rough and leaves 'em, the eternal rider who has no responsibilities beyond himself and his horse, who shows no emotion and never weeps, whose answer to the world is his drawn pistol—this is the image which I believe has created weak, blustering males. For men are not really like that. Men have the same deep emotions that women have, they are capable of a profound tenderness, which expressed in male terms can create happiness in love and friendship and parental relationships. They are capable of tears and should not be ashamed of them; and are not ashamed in older and more sophisticated societies than ours. They are subject to human feelings and moods and the need for love and approval. Often they are called upon to be independent too young, to assume the stature of men when they are not yet men, and this early demand, this fear of being "sissy," produces a man with a deep inferiority complex, one who cannot understand love or really love a woman, because he hates himself and fears secretly that he does not live up to the he-man image.

And subconsciously women feel this lack in the men they marry, and when their sons are born they are divided between shaping them into the sort of men they dream of, and shaping them into the common male image, whom they cannot really love. The result is an emotional ambivalence in a mother. She knows the sort of man a woman needs, for she personally hates the he-man, and yet, fearful of being blamed, she allows and even encourages her son toward "he-manism," lest he be thought effeminate. The truth is that the ability to love should be a vital part of every man and woman, the man to love as a man with all the glory of his maleness not only in body but in mind and spirit, and woman to love in all the glory of her femaleness in the trinity of body, mind and spirit. The ability to love with tenderness and loyalty is natural to both, and nothing is more despicable than the false "toughness" which our society has foisted upon men. They must have the courage to repudiate it as false to masculinity. How much our American culture has lost by our men fearing to be thought effeminate if they are interested in arts and letters, or even educated and cultivated! Fortunately, we have taken a turn for the better, thanks to the new discoveries in science, which put a premium on the superior brain and make education essential at the highest levels. The modern respect for brains will illuminate and uplift our whole society, pervading it with new spirit and energy and enjoyment. For, let's face it, most men do not enjoy being primitive and belonging to an age now obsolete. We are no longer pioneers, men or women, and it is boring to pretend that the past still lives, except as a brief era which compelled the harsh cruelties of pioneer existence.

We need a new look at men and at women in this modern age. The old hostilities may now be discarded. Men no longer keep women in subjection, and women do not wish to intimidate men by their new-found freedom. An atmosphere of mutual trust and respect should be the modern attitude, and out of it should come new discovery. There are new pleasures to be found, based upon new understanding between men and women. Yes, our society is changing very fast. The old rules and traditions no longer hold. It may even be that we need a new sort of marriage. Let us make our conclusions later, however. At present we are in the stage of discontent, of restlessness, of breaking the rules and casting aside traditions. The result of this disturbance is the change in sex mores, the destruction of family life, and the neglected child.

III

What Is a Neglected Child?

What is a neglected child? He is a child not planned for, not wanted. Neglect begins, therefore, before he is born. His parents are guilty, angry, resentful at his coming. He enters the world under a shadow. It is impossible for the parents, whether married or not, to hide their feelings. In a hundred small ways they show it without knowing it. Reason, or even conscience, may tell them that it is not fair to the child to live in the shadow of their wish that he not be born. They may, if married, make an honest effort to behave well toward him. They may even become oversolicitous as compensation for lack of love. But they cannot forget his existence and their memories maintain the shadow. If they are not married, the man forgets as best he can; the mother disposes of the child as best she can. About half of the children given for adoption, however, are by married couples.

The New York State Family Court Act, which became effective September, 1962, in providing for the termination of parental rights, makes the following definition of a neglected child:

"Section 611 defines a permanently neglected child as a person under eighteen years of age who has been placed in the care of an authorized agency and whose parent or custodian has failed for a period of more than one year following placement . . . to maintain contact with and plan for the future of the child, although physically and financially able to do so, notwithstanding the agency's diligent efforts to encourage and strengthen the parental relationship."

This does not, of course, take into account the child neglected in the home; that child must suffer until in some extremity neighbors notice and report his case. It relates solely to that vast group of children in orphanages and detention homes and places for delinquents, among whom there are some who could benefit from adoption. I amend the word *some* and make the sentence read, ". . . most of whom could benefit from adoption," the number unknown, either of the ones who could benefit from adoption or the ones presently confined in institutions.

I am perhaps peculiarly sensitive to the fact that we have so many children held in orphanages and institutions, for having spent so much of my life abroad, I see that we sin more than other peoples in this respect. Then, too, I have more than the average number of visitors in my home from abroad and perhaps they speak to me more frankly than they would to average Americans. At any rate, they never fail to be shocked at the number of our children held in institutions here in the United States and they ask very piercing questions as to the reason for this. I have myself asked those questions and I find the answers unsatisfactory. I share the feelings of my visitors on the subject of orphanages and institutions. No institution is good enough for a child, nor can it possibly replace the normal home he should have. I recognize the fact that since we have the small-family system, and relatives assume little or no responsibility—as I personally think they should, even if they must be helped to do so—there are children who need shelter temporarily, either because their families cannot be reunited or because the children are too old for adoption. But their limited num-

ber does not account for the many small children I
see in orphanages throughout our country. I am glad
to note that these orphanages are diminishing in number, for the public is being awakened to concede the
established fact that the orphanage and the hospital are
not proper places for healthy children.

Though we recognize it, though it is acknowledged,
still too little is being done about it. Change in human
situations involving responsibility is always slow.
Then, too, there are those who benefit by the *status
quo* and so are reluctant to move to a new situation,
which may have no place for them. The immense
amount of money now petrified in huge buildings is in
itself an inducement to continue to fill these buildings
with children who have nowhere to go. Administrators
from high to low are comfortable in their jobs, and
unless they are unusually conscientious they will op-
pose change which may throw them out of work even
temporarily. The very fact that there is a place where
children without homes can be sheltered and fed is a
temptation to maintain such refuges for the lost and
the displaced. Until and unless some better system is
organized and stabilized, the orphanage as an institution
is likely to continue indefinitely. Nor am I satisfied to
be told that it is gradually disappearing. It should dis-
appear altogether and speedily. If temporary homes are

needed, as of course they are for children whose families are not permanently scattered or irresponsible, then they should be something very different from orphanages. A stigma is attached to the word orphanage. It is still true that some sort of disgusting sense of charity is attached to the very idea. Certain trade and service groups maintain orphanages for children of their deceased members, religious groups maintain orphanages so that children of their dead or scattered members may be reared in a certain religion. Whatever the reason, the child in any orphanage is there not for his own sake but for the sake of some organization, and is thereby deprived of his natural right to home and family.

Various tests and studies have been made on the development of children growing up in orphanages. These show that few children emerge from the experience without damage to their emotional and intellectual growth. The lack of individual care even where there is adequate food and clothing and housing, the lack of centralization of concern through the relationship to one or two parents, so essential for the wellbeing of a child, result in a stunted personality. In other words, no orphanage can provide the natural setting into which a child should be born, the primary closeness to the mother in babyhood and early childhood, and the security and confidence in the strength and protection of the father. A loving family experience teaches a child to love, and unless this is learned early, the individual grows up either unloving and self-centered or clinging and dependent upon anyone who shows the slightest sign of affection. The proper balance is not maintained. Then, too, in orphanage life the opportunities for education are limited. All too soon the child is thrust into the world to earn his living as best he can without sufficient attention to his gifts and natural skills.

In spite of this, orphanages exist, although fortunately in decreasing numbers. Visit any orphanage, then look at the children and ask why they are not adopted, and the answer will be that they are not free for adoption. Ask why they are not free for adoption and the reply will be that some parent or other relative is not willing to give the child up. At first this may seem a plausible answer. But upon thought one is impelled to ask still another question. Why, if there is so much attachment, does not this parent or other relative provide a home for the child and thereby remove from him the stigma of being in an orphanage? For, I repeat, there is a stigma to being the inmate of an orphanage. Administrators, teachers and other personnel may enjoy a certain status by helping to maintain a charity.

"It is wonderful of you to take care of the poor little orphans" may be pleasing to such ears. But there is nothing wonderful to the orphan in being so cared for. On the contrary, it is a handicap to him and always will be. When he goes out into the world, the orphanage cannot possibly serve as a family for him, however kindly he may have been treated there. "He grew up in an orphanage" means he has no family, no standing, he is alone in the world, he was saved by charity. Do not mistake me. I doubt very much that the orphan is treated with overt cruelty. He is nevertheless being cruelly treated by life itself. He is a deprived person. He has little or no chance to develop his true personality.

Who is responsible for his condition? Society is responsible. We have not yet learned how to control the effects of the industrial age into which we have been so rapidly catapulted. Only a few decades ago eighty percent of the population of the United States was farming. Today eight percent are farmers, and that is too many. We are producing too much food. The present goal of government is to reduce the number to five percent. With modern methods of farming and with the industrialization of farming itself so that it, too, has become an industry, five percent may be too many. In this short space of time the rural family, the big family unit, wherein young and old were needed on the farm, has been reduced to the two-parent family, with other relatives not responsible for the children of any two members. This means that the only persons presently responsible for orphans are the two parents. If they are dead the children are free for adoption unless a relative decides to accept responsibility, and this he may not do. He may merely refuse to yield the child for adoption, and thereby condemn him to being a perpetual orphan. The law has until very recently insisted that blood kin owns the child, like property, whether the child is happy and well cared for or not. This is an injustice to the public, as well as to the child, for when a parent or other relative refuses to allow a child to be adopted, without assuming any responsibility for maintenance, he himself makes use of public charity, although he often uses family pride as a reason for not allowing the child to be given for adoption.

It is slowly being recognized, however, among those who have the child's welfare at heart, that this dead hand of the irresponsible parent or relative must not be allowed to destroy a child's chances for a better life. As mentioned previously, in 1962 the Family Court Act became effective in New York State. Under Section 611 the court has the original jurisdiction to put an end to the custody over the child for the reason of permanent neglect. Before proceeding, however, the agency must be able to allege that the child is a person under eighteen years of age, that the agency is a properly authorized agency, that the agency has made every possible effort to maintain and strengthen the parental ties, and must moreover describe the efforts that have been made. The agency must also declare that in spite of all such efforts the parent or custodian has failed to maintain a proper relationship with the child, or to plan for his future, although physically and financially able to do so. Therefore, the agency must declare, it is in the moral and temporal interests of the child that the custody be terminated.

Presumably the child is now free for adoption. Nothing moves so fast, however, where the law is concerned. After such an allegation is filed, the court may arrange for a copy of it and a summons to be sent out, demanding that the parent or custodian show cause why the court should not terminate the custody and award it to the petitioner, who is the authorized agency. Provision follows with due notice of right to counsel and a fair hearing. At the adjudicatory hearing the court must be satisfied that the allegations are true, that is, that they are supported by factual evidence, which is to be limited only to competent, material and relevant facts. Only then may the court begin a dispositional hearing, with reports to be treated as confidential. After the dispositional hearing the court may decide whether to terminate the custody of the parent or guardian over the child permanently, or to give a suspended judgment. Under the suspended judgment the parent must promise to maintain regular contact with the child and show evidence of real interest in the child's welfare and development. The said parent or child must plan with the agency for the child's future, and if it is financially possible, the parent must share in the cost. Meanwhile the parent must prepare a proper home for the child.

When this law was passed, it was hoped that the voluntary agencies who have children under their care would review all the cases and see how many could benefit by the termination of parental custody and exchange the endless foster care for adoptive homes. Such hope has been unfulfilled. There has been very little activity of this sort by authorized agencies, we are told. Indeed, long before the Act of 1962, under the social welfare law in New York, if a child placed with an agency was not visited for a year, a legal guardian could be appointed for him on the grounds of abandonment. It seems, however, that either under the new law or the old one, both public and voluntary agencies have been very slow to move toward freeing a child for adoption. Public welfare bodies are fearful even of accepting the surrender of a child from an unwed mother unless a definite adoptive family is ready to receive it. A proper concern for public funds is praise-worthy, but in this case the unwed mother often gets discouraged, gradually ceases to visit her child and eventually drifts away. The child then is definitely abandoned and yet is not free for adoption. There is also the chance that the mother, not allowed to sur-render her child when she wishes to do so, may become so emotionally tied to the child that she cannot sur-render it, even when there is a good adoptive family ready. Again the child is left in limbo. One must con-clude upon ample evidence that agencies caring for children in the State of New York do not, except in unusual cases, take advantage of their right to termi-nate parental custody where it would serve the child's interests to be adopted. This is true in spite of the fact that in a self-survey by fourteen agencies, who cared for seventeen thousand children as of the year 1955, it was declared that for nineteen percent of the children, adoption would have been the best plan.

One may well ask, Why the lethargy?, for I believe it is lethargy rather than ill intent or even vested interest. An agency is a slow-moving body, large or small. It gets into a rut of activity—or inactivity—and it is difficult to change one rut for another. The slow-grinding mill of receiving a child, placing the child under institutional or foster care, providing for its food, shelter and clothing, making the usual inspections and writing the usual reports—all constitute an easy, accepted and seemingly rational procedure. But time passes swiftly, especially in the life of a child. An agency has a long life, but in a handful of years, less than a decade, a child is adolescent and the time for adoption is past. One must act quickly if one is to save a child, but agencies do not act quickly, or at least not quickly enough.

Then, as others have pointed out in explaining this lag, the enactment of law and its application through social action occur at different times in any democratic society. A law is enacted when it becomes evident that for the welfare of society it is necessary to have such a law. Its fulfillment through public obedience takes place only when there are enough people who agree with it to obey it and enforce it. Prohibition in our country in the past provides a good example. A law was passed, but enough people disagreed with it so heartily that it never became positive action, except in a negative sense. That is, people disobeyed it and the only positive action was that the law was repealed. It is interesting to observe that exactly the same situation prevails today in modern India. There, also, prohibition is a law, but people are reacting by making and selling illicit liquor, and to drink has become a sign of social status, so much so that many people are drinking who never before did so. Sooner or later India too will repeal the law, which, it seems, cannot pass into social action.

To take another example, the mentally retarded and even the mentally ill, it is now being recognized, reach their best development or recovery in the community rather than in institutions. Leaders in this field are repudiating institutional concealment except in severe cases and are urging rehabilitation in a normal environment. But the community has to be educated to respond to the new responsibility. It has to be taught that the subnormal or abnormal person is an inevitable part of any community, and his welfare and development there are as much his right as are those of any citizen. Slowly the idea is percolating into community thinking, but much more slowly than one wishes and hopes.

In the same way, the increasing responsibility that the courts are assuming over the welfare of neglected children by making laws for the protection of them, is only now beginning to have some slight response in the obligation of the agencies who have the child in their care to release him to the community of normal life through adoption. The courts are aware of the lag and in some states require reports from agencies at the end of a year of placement and subsequent reports thereafter, always with accompanying data and recommendations. As evidence of the lag, however, agencies tend to resent even this requirement, and are making efforts to have it abrogated. It is to be hoped that the courts will not yield to such efforts.

Of course it takes real thought and much work to place a child for adoption, but the truth, too, is that in the past the courts have ordered a child placed with some agency and then have forgotten the child's existence. In 1961 a study was made in New York State of a hundred children chosen at random from among four hundred and thirty-seven who had been placed in foster care. The study was based on an evaluation of the child's adoptability at three times in his life: the first when he entered the agency, the second two years later, and the third at the study date. The standards for adoptability were the quality and degree of family ties, the degree of family adequacy, and the child's ability to adjust to his adopted family, his physical, mental and emotional condition.

This group of one hundred children were of mixed races, sixty of them Negro, thirty of them white and six of them Puerto Rican. Five of the children had been separated from their parents for fourteen years or more. The average length of separation was eight years. Parental neglect was apparent both before and during foster care. Agencies had tried to bring about helpful contact between child and family, but the indifference of the parents was obvious. Parents were contributing financially to the child in only eight cases. Seventy-seven percent of the homes were permanently disorganized with little or no hope of rehabilitation. This had been the case when the children were first placed. There were among the parents some who had moved, others who had disappeared, and yet they still spoke of taking their children home "some day." Of the hundred children selected, forty-eight were born in wedlock, twelve were born to married women outside of wedlock, thirty-eight were born out of wedlock, the status of one child could not be determined, and one child was a foundling. The average age of the children at the time of the study was eleven years and since the median number of years of separation from the parents was eight, it was obvious that the children had been away from their homes for most of their lives, and moreover, when they had been consigned to agency care, they were young enough for easy adoption, so far as age goes.

The reasons for placement with an agency were multiple: neglect in sixty-two cases, destitution in sixty-one cases, parents institutionalized for one reason or another in thirty-nine cases, marital discord in thirty-seven cases, physical incapacity of the parent in eighteen cases, and working parents in fifteen cases. All of the hundred children had been tested and found to be of normal intelligence when placed. Yet after the average period of eight years of foster care, forty-eight had become unstable and twenty-four were diagnosed as severely retarded. The writer of the study speaks of "the emotional no man's land in which they found themselves, which had led them to withdraw from a world that offered only a modicum of warmth and security, or to lash out aggressively among their fellows." At the time of placement by the agency, the study had predicted that thirty-five children were adoptable; forty-two, unadoptable; and twenty-three, unclassifiable. By the time the study was made twelve were judged still adoptable, but of these twelve only two were legally free for adoption. This marked increase in emotional suffering as years passed certainly points to the inadequacy of foster care as a substitute for real family life. And since some of the children were brothers and sisters and were kept unadopted because the agency decided they should stay together, the question arises as to whether it might not have been better for the children to be separated in order that each child might have received true parental care and affection in adoptive homes. The study concludes with the statement: "Immediate, intensive casework leading to an early decision for the best ultimate plan for the child's life is indicated *at the time the child first becomes known to the court or social agency* [italics mine]."

Social agencies, it must be said, are in fact making some effort to evaluate the child when he first appears and to make a life plan for him, either with the natural parents or with adoptive ones. The attitude of courts and judges, however, remains unsatisfactory. The old punitive attitude is evidenced in family courts, and children are removed from parents as punishment rather than for reasons of benefiting the child and possibly rehabilitating the family. All too seldom are the parents given an intensive, coherent, continuing help in their community to establish a proper home situation for the child.

Yet this is, I think, only one aspect of the general indifference toward children in our country. We are very good at helping in crises, we Americans, but our attention span, and indeed our span of interest, are very short when it comes to solving perpetual problems, and most human problems are perpetual. In a study on delinquent children brought to a juvenile court recently in one of our Northern states during a period of three months, it was found that most of the children were not delinquent but were only in need of care and supervision. They were the victims of parental and community neglect. Yet delinquent children, generally speaking, are more fortunate in our society than neglected ones. We have detention homes for delinquents, but even temporary shelters for neglected children are inadequate. Too often the child is sent back to a home where a drunken father, or a mentally ill mother, makes its life a hell. Analysis of old and new cases, one judge writes, show that children brought in as neglected "present the most difficult and long-standing complex of family problems and those with which our present courts are least equipped to deal."

Yet long before the child comes to court, neighbors, schools, hospitals and social agencies in his community know of his circumstances. Long ago they were well aware that something was gravely wrong in the family. And how, it may be asked, can courts with their untrained staffs and heavy case loads be asked to

supervise and correct local situations? Their only recourse is to take the child from the family and place
him with some agency. And even in most grave cases,
such as mental illness, degeneracy, drug addiction and
alcoholism, the court has only the power to make no
more than a temporary placement. Even under the
recent new State Family Court plan in New York, the
first placement must be only for eighteen months, with
authority to extend year by year. Yet it has been
proved by research and experience that for children
more than a year and a half old the likelihood of
returning the child to its natural parents is increasingly
improbable, and even finding an adoptive home, increasingly difficult. The present drive to urge adoptive
families to take children beyond babyhood can
scarcely be called successful, although no final figures
have been set. And it must not be forgotten in the face
of all this that authorized agencies have not as yet been
willing to use their power to terminate parental rights,
even when it is deemed best for the child that they
do so.

Why should agencies be so slow to act? One answer
given is the "many difficulties that an agency faces in
starting court proceedings." These difficulties when
studied resolve themselves into the requirements which

a court makes for full information before deciding to separate a child permanently from its natural family. Yet surely it is not too much to ask that an agency supply this information insofar as it is possible. The court must know how the child has been treated by the parents, whether the parents have any true interest in the child, and what efforts the agency is making or has made to better the relationship between parents and child. The real difficulty, I fear, is not in presenting the information, but in the inadequacy of the services the agency offers in helping the parents and in planning for the child. It is true, however, that it is within the power of judges, who may or may not be adequately trained to evaluate information, to decide on emotional grounds to give the natural parents "another chance," and the relentless and unreasonable determination of some judges never to separate a child from its natural family is of no help, either, in the general situation of neglected children. But of judges I shall speak later. Suffice it to say here that they are the weakest point in our legal chain. Meanwhile we need new laws that will enlarge and clarify the power of our courts to terminate unhealthy parent-child relationships. We need new laws, too, to define the duties of all authorized agencies, which must include real and not token services to parents as soon as a child is taken from its home by the court. Such agencies should report regularly and often to the court, so that valuable time is not wasted. A year in a child's life is a long time, but it goes quickly for the agency. A few years pass, and it may be too late for the child to be saved.

IV

The Community Responsibility (and Welcome House)

Where is the answer? Again it is in the community. What is the answer? The answer is that the community must take the place of the old large-family unit. The community must assume responsibility for each child within its confines. Not one must be neglected, whatever his condition. The community must see that every child gets the advantages and opportunities which are due him as a citizen and as a human being. It is paradoxical and absurd that a community under present federal, state and local laws will do little or nothing to maintain a child in his own family home, and yet, when he is orphaned or displaced by some unfortunate circumstances, will spend more and more money as his placement makes return to normal life in his community less and less likely or possible. Thus we add only sixty cents a day as an allowance for an additional child in a home that needs aid, but pay two to three dollars for that same child in a foster home, five to seven dollars for the child in an institution, and from ten to twenty-one dollars for that same child when he has become so emotionally disturbed that he needs residential treatment services.

Instead of this horrible waste of public funds, our communities must discover this child before he leaves his own home, and must do everything they can to help the child's own family to solve its problems and mend its ways so as to provide a proper home environment for the child. The only substitute would be a very great increase in adoptive homes. We talk a great deal, we Americans, about home life and "togetherness" and such fine-sounding truths, but we do very little about it for the ones who are most needy. There is a monstrous discrepancy here. And if we are to substitute adoptive homes on a large scale, again the community must create new and more effective services.

"All of us who have worked in agencies," the head of a fine adoption agency writes, "have seen how, when we have changed our own attitudes and enlarged our services, we have found many children adoptable who were formerly left throughout their childhood and youth in institutions or in a series of foster homes. We have found that children up to fourteen years of age, children with limited sight, deafness, heart conditions, palsy, and children with mixed racial background could be placed and become part of happy loving families. We have also learned that the statement saying that the courts never permitted a placement across racial and even religious lines was not correct when the evidence showed that this was the only practicable placement and was clearly in the best interest of the child. Law may be regarded as the public acceptance of the position to which the social conscience aspires, even when the aspiration is still in large part an ideal. It cannot, however, be expected to reflect sanction of an ideal service, which is neither realized nor even part of the true aspirations of the community."

Community responsibility begins before the child is removed from its home and placed for adoption. The degree of parental instability must be observed before it damages the child, and measures be taken to discover the cause of the instability and to remove it if possible. In short, every effort must be made in the community to help the disturbed family, much as in the old large-family days an erring or disturbed member was immediately surrounded, coaxed, coerced as needed, into performing his duty. If he was ill and incapable, other members took over the tasks necessary for the child's welfare until the parents could function again. Thus the child was disturbed as little as possible. In the study of the one hundred children mentioned above, it was revealed that before the children were removed from their homes, all the homes except one had major problems. Seventy-seven of the children had suffered family disorganization so grave that there was little or no hope of rehabilitation. In other words, the community had done nothing for these families until it was too late, and too late meant the children had to be taken from the homes.

I remind myself here that of the hundred children in the study I have previously described, seventy were considered unadoptable at the time of the study, and of these, forty-eight were judged to have emotional disturbance sufficiently severe so that they could not form new family ties. This emotional disturbance had increased markedly since 'the separation from their parents. The separation was more than physical, for most of the parents were not interested in the children. Only thirteen mothers had participated in the children's placement plans, although it is significant to note that twenty-one fathers so participated. Thirteen parents had remarried, but only four of these even considered having the child returned to the home, and never went further than talking about it. The separation in such cases, then, was so complete that the child should have been placed early for adoption. Court action would have been needed, for in spite of no intention of providing a home for their children, forty-eight of the parents, or nearly half, would not free the children legally for adoption. There were three major bases for court action, mental illness and neglect being the two most important, and desertion the third. Yet nothing was done.

If the community is to assume responsibility for family stability, as I believe it should, the question arises as to how this can be accomplished. The community in our society is loosely organized, without central source of authority, and without general responsibility. Of agencies with specific responsibilities we have plenty and too many, since usually their efforts are unco-ordinated. There is an organization of some sort for every handicap, every activity, every religious persuasion, even for every diversion and amusement.

But there is no central source of authority, no watchful power ready, whose duty is to discover the ailing members of society. The ailing member is on his own; he may turn to this specific agency or that for help, but unless he has the specific ill necessary for their interest he is thrown back on himself. Thus he becomes a disturbing force, first in his own family and then in the community. When his ill has developed into insanity, drunkenness, bankruptcy, he draws some attention to his needs and the effect this personal disintegration has had on his family. Until he has reached this point of no return, however, very little is done for him or even known about him, and by that time it is too late. Every child displaced from its home is a repetition of the sad words, Too late—too late! The final punishment is always on the child.

What is the answer to the question, Who is responsible? Where is the power to save the lost child by saving his home and his parents? At present the only hope is in some child welfare agency. Here is the process:

The child is taken from his home and placed with an agency by some court. Thus he enters into a strange new world. What is this agency? What are these agencies that have to do with children? They were created by someone out of a special need, a child's need of home, care and protection, a child's need to find safety and security. Agencies grow, as all things grow, out of a nebula of distress and need and conviction gathering into a focus of action. It is the way that stars are made in the heavens and the way that great music is composed and great books written. It is an act of creation. Each agency has its own impulse of beginning, its own special purpose of performing. Some are created by government and are therefore public agencies, some are created by private individuals and are therefore private agencies. But private agencies must conform to government standards and must be approved by government, and it is so decreed in most states of the Union.

I can best illustrate the creation of a private agency by telling the history of Welcome House, Inc., an approved agency in my own state of Pennsylvania. And the reason I choose this agency as an illustration is that I had a part in creating it, although at no time of my life had I ever thought of such a thing as founding an adoption agency. But one day, a day some fifteen years ago, the need arose. Two small babies were suddenly and unexpectedly presented to me as gifts from heaven, unprecedented gifts. These were special babies. The mothers of both babies were young

American white women and the father of one was East Indian; of the other, Chinese.

How well I remember the day I first heard of them! It was December and Christmas was in the air. I had been busy with shopping and gift-wrapping and I had let the mail pile up on my desk. Then, horrified at the accumulation, I went to my office after the household was in bed and asleep and began the task of opening and sorting. Somewhere in the heap was a long white envelope from an adoption agency. And why, I wondered, would an adoption agency write to me now? Our children were nearly grown and we had no thought of adding to our family. I tore the envelope open and unfolded the sheet of paper within. It was a letter from a distant adoption agency.

"Can you help us?" the letter inquired. "We consider this the finest child we have ever had in the agency."

It was my first acquaintance with Robbie. There before my eyes were the bare facts of his brief life: age, fifteen months; father, East Indian; mother, American white; intelligence, excellent; ancestry, impeccable; skin color, brown.

I read on. How had he been born? Why was this finest of children a mixed-blood child? His was a love story. A man, an American missionary with his missionary wife, driven by the love of Christ, had gone years ago to India to preach a gospel of love—the fatherhood of God, the brotherhood of man. Their children, born in India, believed what their parents preached. The young daughter, nurtured upon faith, fell in love with a young East Indian when she grew out of childhood, and he, taking the white man's creed as truth, loved her. This the missionary had not foreseen. He did not mean "that kind of love." He could not realize that belief in the fatherhood of God and the brotherhood of man leads to all love. So the two young people were separated and the young mother was brought back to her homeland to bear her child. And the child, because he had not where to lay his head when he was born into this world, was put out for adoption, but no one wanted him.

I acknowledge it was indignation and not love that made me get on the telephone. One after another I called all my Indian friends, and then, any friend remotely interested in India. It was true. No one wanted Robbie. There were many reasons but this was the fact. I could, perhaps, have taken more time to discover somewhere the possible parents who were looking for a little boy, whether his skin was white or brown. Alas, there was no time. In a few days, the letter had said, Robbie would have to go to a Negro orphanage. "Not

that we have any prejudice," the kind social worker
hastened to add. "It's just that we can't get him into a
white one. Yet it seems a pity to put the burden of
prejudice on a little boy, if he can escape it." The people of India, I must explain, are Caucasian—not that it
matters, either.

In the burst of indignation, now extended, I called
up the agency and told them that we would take the
baby, not to adopt, I was sorry to say, for my husband and I were long past the approved age for adoption, but we would at least care for Robbie until we
found parents for him. The good social worker in
reply warned me that there was little hope for that,
for she had written to every state in the Union, and
to Hawaii as well, but with no results. She had even
appealed to the Indian embassy in Washington, where
a voice replied, rather caustically, that there were
thousands of such children in India as a result of centuries of colonization, and perhaps this one child could
be cared for in the United States. "Never mind," I
said, still angry, "bring him anyway."

One night, deep in the darkness, the doorbell rang
and there stood the good woman with a little boy in a
red snowsuit in her arms. He was sucking his thumb
and his eyes were huge and tragic, with the look that
always reveals a child without home and parents. I took

him in my arms, and he was as motionless in the arms of a stranger as a bird is in the hand of a human being.

"I'm sorry I can't stay," the good woman said. "But you'll understand."

She went away and Robbie's eyes did not change. He knew that it did not matter who came or went. He belonged to nobody. At that moment anger faded from my heart and love began. I took him upstairs to my own room, I undressed him and bathed him warm and clean and put on a pair of woolly pajamas that I had found in the attic chest. He uttered not a sound, he did not make a move to protest. He did not cry. It was I who cried because he was so desperately brave. I rocked him awhile and he looked at me with those great dark eyes, wondering who I was and why he was here. I put him in the crib beside my bed, and he lay, not sleeping, but sucking his thumb again. When I was ready for bed, I turned on the night light so that he could see me and know that I was ready for his small brown hand, extended tentatively through the bars of the crib. Again and again that little hand came toward me in the night, and each time I received it into my own.

Of course I could not sleep. I could not sleep for remembering all those little children that I had seen in other countries. Yes, India was full of them, the sons and daughters of Englishmen and Indian women. I had seen them in China, too, and Indonesia, and Indo-China and the islands of the sea, wherever white men had gone in their youth and energy. The children were beautiful, nearly always more handsome and more intelligent than either side of their ancestry, and nearly always wasted, as this child had been wasted. Neither side claimed them. And informed now by love, anger came flooding back again. This must not happen in my own country. Something must be done about it. There were other children, possibly no, probably yes. Where were they and how could I find them?

I had not long to wait. If you ask me how it all happened, I can only reply that the increasing wisdom of our modern scientists is revealing new and wonderful knowledge to us all. We are told that throughout the universe there is the strange, inescapable element of chance. Causality and determinism, those twin pillars of fate and predestination, are no longer reliable excuses for human behavior, it seems. Chance is an inescapable constant. I mention this here because quite by chance I had another baby given to me within the next five days, another little boy, named Peter. He was only nine days old, and I went to the hospital where he was waiting, and I brought him home. Again it was a love story, love between a young Chinese man, a brilliant student, and an American girl, and again neither family could accept the result of love. For me Peter was the answer to my question—were there other children of such love? The answer was yes, at least there were some, and certainly they were in need.

The two little boys, arrived in our house from nowhere, brought into play yet another force now being vaguely defined by scientists. It is the element of free will. Life is unpredictable for human beings, but its very unpredictability provides opportunity for mind to shape destiny. We are not ruled by inescapable, immutable universal law. We have freedom to choose what to do with what we have. What I had was two little boys, who by their very existence convinced me that there were others. I was naïve enough at this point to believe what I had been told: that nobody wanted to adopt mixed-blood children. Upon this premise I proceeded toward the first stage of Welcome House, Inc. I would find a good and kind family in my neighborhood, a couple much younger than my husband and I, and I would ask them to be parents to the two babies, and we would be grandparents. As other children came, we could, hopefully, find other families. Meanwhile we could help with the children's support and persuade our friends to help. Ours is a friendly community, founded upon the precepts of Quakers and

Mennonites. I did take the precaution, however, of consulting the leaders in the community. Our general storekeeper, the owner of our village garage, the local superintendent of schools, the minister and other good citizens came to our house one night and we talked the plan over. I explained about the mixed-blood children in Asia, and what their hardships are. I said I could not bear to have the same thing happen here. I described their beauty, I quoted the hybrid corn, the hybrid rose. They listened, and when all had been said and heard, our storekeeper spoke in his stout Pennsylvania-Dutch accent: "Ve nodt only vant them, ve vill be proudt to have them."

So Welcome House began. In this first stage it was just a house, a big white farmhouse next door to our own house. Friends helped us to buy it, for it did not belong to me, and by that time, five months after the babies came to us, we had found the parents, a Pennsylvania-Dutch couple, respected and beloved in our community, he a high school teacher and she a wife and mother, both twenty years younger than we were. The acquaintance began between parents and children. One day when I saw Robbie climb into the father's lap and Peter hold out his arms to the mother, I knew the time had come. The family was ready. Friends helped to furnish the house, the couple contributed their belongings, and life began again. Within a year or two, nine mixed-blood children belonged to the family, the youngest a little Korean baby, born in the United States, the eldest an American-Chinese boy of fifteen and with him his younger sister and brother. The community enjoyed the children, our schools and churches accepted them, and all was well.

Except that more children kept coming! We did no publicity, feeling that we must not grow too fast, but still the children came, most of them babies, but older children too, who were orphaned or deserted and did not "fit," whatever that means! One family was big enough and we began another, with a second young couple. Soon that family had five children.

It was Lennie who now convinced me that mixed-blood children could be adopted. For where was there a baby like Lennie? He was handed to me, five months old, at the railroad station in Chicago when I was passing on my way home from a westward journey. We recognized each other instantly. He smiled at me and I adored him. I took him from the arms of a social worker and hurried on my way to the train and brought him home with me. I was sad that I could not be his mother myself. For this child was so gay, so alert, so aware that I knew from the moment I saw him that he was no ordinary human being. I knew, too, that the real barrier to the adoption of mixed-blood children was not that no one wanted them, but that adoption practice at that time demanded child and adoptive parents to match, and it was usually impossible to find the exact match. But did it matter whether there was such matching? Who really matches his parents? The genes that carry the master plan of any human being may be given him by distant, even unknown, ancestors and not by his parents. Looking at Lennie, I resolved to ignore the whole business of matching in race and religion, and find parents worthy of him, whatever their race or religion. Lennie stayed in our house for three months while I searched for his adoptive parents.

One night I had a speech to make. A vast audience sat in a hall, a crowd of well-dressed, comfortable people. Our is such a community. I thought to myself, "Surely someone here wants Lennie." So before I began my speech, which was on quite another subject, I told his simple story. It was a love story again—the story of an American soldier in Japan who fell in love with a beautiful Japanese girl, married her and brought her home with him. She died when Lennie was born and, heartbroken, the young father gave his child for adoption because his own family would not receive him.

"Is there no young couple here who would like to

have Lennie for their own?" This was the concluding question to my appeal. The next day I had one letter. It was from a young Presbyterian minister who was finishing his seminary training. He and his wife wanted Lennie.

We began our acquaintance. I had to make very sure that Lennie would like his new parents and that they were worthy of him. This took a month more, and in the meantime, I said to the young minister, "You know that it is possible that a half-Japanese son may be a handicap to you in getting a pastorate?"

"I have thought of that," he replied.

At the end of the month Lennie went home to his parents. Here I must tell the end of the story. For when he had his degree, the young minister applied for a job in a pastorate in his home state, California. When all the preliminaries were over and he had only to wait for acceptance or rejection, the reply came. It went something like this:

"We have reduced the applications to two, yours and another young man's. There is nothing to choose between you. Both of you are well prepared to be our pastor. We see by your application sheet, however, that you have adopted a little half-Japanese son. You are the man we want." I tell this story to balance the beginning of Robbie's story. There are Christians and Christians.

Once we found that people did want to adopt the mixed-blood babies and once we took the firm stand that parents must not be rejected on grounds of non-matching race and religion, the rest was easy. A group of our citizens formed a board of directors and we made formal application to the State of Pennsylvania to set up a private adoption agency. We found the officials sympathetic and circumspect. Were we sure there were enough such children born in the United States to warrant an agency especially for them? We asked them to make their own investigation. They wrote to all state agencies to inquire. The replies showed that while there were not mixed-blood children in great numbers, nevertheless they constituted the chief problem for adoption agencies. There were simply no prospective parents for such children.

We were granted our charter at once after that. It was a charter like none other, perhaps, in the world, for it permits Welcome House, Inc., to receive and place for adoption children from any state in the Union, born in the United States but of Asian or part-Asian ancestry. We set up a modest office, employed two social workers of experience and warm heart, and two other workers equally devoted, to carry on the business of Welcome House, Inc. From then on there were no more problems—no big ones, that is. There are always problems with adoption, generally speaking. Our laws are confused and contradictory, and often it is as difficult to place a child for adoption in another state as though it were another country.

Otherwise the course of Welcome House has run with amazing smoothness as the years have passed. Our children in the two families of our first stage grew up happily. The eldest now are married, self-supporting and good citizens. The others are still in our public schools. I do not believe our community is unique, even in its acceptance of our children, but it is true that they do accept the children with a warmth entirely natural, neither too little nor too much, so that the children do not feel singular or special. The time came when, like all other agencies, we had more parents who wanted the mixed-blood children than we had children. The barriers have broken down, not only for us, but for other agencies as well. For it was an integral part of our policy to help other agencies do what we were doing. Indeed, our directors said, the sooner they did it, the sooner we could go out of business. Out of that policy grew what we call our referral system. It is nothing formidable. It is simply that when parents apply to us from other states we keep their names on file if we have no child available, and more often than not, sooner or later we get a letter from an agency in a state asking if we will accept a mixed-blood child for placement. Then we search our files and reply that while of course we will accept any such child, nevertheless they may like to know that in their own state such-and-such persons have applied to us for a mixed-blood child. In this way we bring child and potential parents together, and the other agency then carries on. Once such a child is successfully placed, the agency does not approach us again, and we have the comforting conviction that they have broken their own barriers of race and religion.

Is our job done? One thing leads to another. Now comes our third stage. We saw other difficult-to-place children here in the United States, the orphaned child, the lonely handicapped child. They need parents, too. We applied to our state authorities to have our charter enlarged to cover any child who might need home and parents. This was granted, and what joy it was to see a little girl, nearly blind, go to gentle and loving parents, who could afford treatment for her, and another child, deaf, go to parents whose hearts were warm and ready, and a little boy, badly burned and scarred, to parents ready and eager to provide for him, and so on. For the heart-warming truth is that if we search carefully enough, there are always people with warm hearts, who will accept a child and make him their own. I know now that there are no unadoptable children.

None? Well, perhaps one exception must be made. The child whose mixture is Negro and white is still too often homeless when he is orphaned by death or desertion. Are such children to be without home and parents? There are not enough Negro families able to adopt them. Yet there are many white families who long for children and for whom there are none. Well, a baby is a baby, isn't he? And there are none sweeter and more lovable than these little mixed-blood babies! Can a brown baby grow up happily in a white family? We have found here at Welcome House that they can. White families have adopted pure Chinese children, pure Japanese children, pure Korean children, all born in the United States. White fathers and mothers love these children so that they become one flesh. Chinese and Japanese families have adopted half-white children, and learned to love them in the same way. Time and again we have proved that race and religion do not matter. All that matters is the ability to love. I know, for I have tried it myself. My own youngest child is half-Negro, born of an American Negro father in Germany and a German mother. Yes, the first few days perhaps I did notice when I bathed her that her skin was darker than my own. The first day perhaps I felt it was strange. But caring for that little body, watching the keen quick mind awaken and develop, enjoying the gaiety and the vigor of the personality, soon made the child my own. Her flesh became my flesh by love, and we are mother and child. Does she fit into our home? Yes, because she is so much like me. I see myself when I was a child in so many of her ways. I could not have created a child more like me than she is, because we have the same kind of mind and heart. Parenthood has nothing to do with color, race or religion. It has to do with far deeper likeness of mind and heart and soul.

So I can dream of a day, perhaps nearer than I think, when childless parents will take a child for their own without caring what the color of the skin may be. On that day prejudice will really be ended and the ultimate reach of love achieved.

V

The Agency Story

Every agency has its own story. Religious organizations found agencies in order that babies without homes may be reared in what they consider is the right religious atmosphere. Organizations of businessmen found orphanages or agencies to care for the children of their members who may be deprived of their homes. Among the religious groups the Catholic are the most insistent upon children of Catholics being adopted by Catholic families, and of the many such agencies I chose one that is fairly typical. It is an agency in a large city, near which I live. It is a good agency, within the rigidities of religion. The atmosphere of any agency is apparent the moment one steps inside the door. This one is kindly and much more casual than most city agencies. Even the building is informal, and when you enter you find the people friendly and offhand in their approach. The agency is headed by a priest, himself kind and even genial. There is no hesitancy in answering questions or in talking about the work of the agency. The most difficult problem in this Catholic agency, Monsignor says, is the placement of Negro children. Very few Negroes today adopt children, and the agency is trying to discover the reason for this. Part of it perhaps is the reluctance on the part of many Negroes to sign legal documents, committing them to obligations which through the insecurity of their lives they may not be able to fulfill.

But the good Monsignor in the Catholic agency continues to answer questions in his own way. Yes, he says, the Negro child is their chief problem. There was once an interagency committee called "Adopt a Child," but it is now out of business for lack of funds. Questions and answers go on in the usual procession:

"How old are most of the infants when you do place them in adoptive homes?"

"About three months old."

"Would you place a child in a home where one parent was not a Catholic?"

"No, we have enough applicants where both man and wife are Catholics and we feel that this is preferable. We have many more applicants than we have babies and we have to eliminate couples in some ways."

"Getting back to institutions, tell me something about the Catholic institutions."

"They are usually specialized, some care for older children, some care for children with particular physical handicaps, some care for children with emotional or psychological handicaps."

"What education or training do these youngsters receive?"

"The institutions for older children offer academic programs and vocational programs. Most children in institutions are high school 'dropouts.' The exceptional child who wants to go on to college has a real problem. He can rarely go out of the city to college. There are just not enough funds available. Most of these youngsters work their way through city colleges, usually going to school at night. Sometimes children in foster homes are helped by their foster parents to go through college."

"What happens to the youngsters after they leave the institutions?"

"There are after-care programs for these young people, called 'opportunity homes,' something between foster homes and furnished rooms."

"Do most of the unwed mothers surrender their children for adoption?"

"The 'tribal' groups keep their illegitimate children, but as people become sophisticated there is more of a social stigma attached to illegitimacy. Also, among the less educated, less sophisticated people there is a stronger sense of family ties. I remember when among the poor Irish here in this city it was not uncommon for a family in Ireland to send over a cousin or niece to live with relatives for a while. You rarely see this any more among the Irish; as they have prospered they have become more formal, less casual about offering hospitality to relatives. Now it is the Negroes and Puerto Ricans who care for children of relatives, and fewer mothers surrender their children in these groups."

"Do you try to see the father of the babies you place? Is any responsibility placed on him?"

"Occasionally we see the father and then he participates in planning for the baby. Usually he flees."

"Do you feel that many children are not placed in

adoptive homes because they cannot be placed in homes of another religion?"

"No, children are not kept from adoption because of religious restrictions, this is a fallacy. We have more Catholic applicants than we have babies. There are more than enough Catholic parents for the Catholic children who need adoptive homes."

"Do you place children other than Catholic children?"

"No."

"What do most people desire in an adopted child?"

"Most people want a child of their own nationality, a child who will 'fit into their home.' Many ask for a child who will resemble them. We try to discourage overemphasis on physical likeness. We feel that parents should recognize that there is a difference between the adopted child and the natural child, and that they should not try to deceive themselves or the child."

"What proportion of the couples who apply to your agency for a child are successful?"

"Approximately one out of six."

"Is there an age limit for adoptive parents?"

"Yes, forty for women, forty-five for men."

"What is the average length of time between a couple's original application and placement of a child?"

"About nine to twelve months. The shortest amount of time is nine months, the maximum is a year and a half—and this is too long. We try to let people know within the first month if they are going to be rejected; we do not want to prolong the agony."

"Do you co-operate with other adoption agencies in the placement of children?"

"We co-operate with the other Catholic agencies; otherwise we do not often work with other agencies."

"Will you place an adopted child in a home where there is already a natural child?"

"Rarely—there are too many childless couples applying; but we will and do place more than one adopted child with a family."

"How many children will you place with a family?"

"We used to place no more than two children with a family unless they were willing to adopt a child with a slight handicap, and then if we thought that they were a good family for this child, we would let them take him as well. Now we place three children if a couple wishes to adopt and can support them. Handicapped children usually go to exceptional people, not to people who are willing to take second best. We have placed three and four handicapped children with a family."

"Do you feel that adopted children have more emotional problems in adolescence than natural children?"

"Adoption is an aggravating cause, not a root cause, of adolescent problems; it can be an added reason for insecurity if the child is already insecure."

"Are there many Catholic children raised in orphanages?"

"There are no longer orphanages where a baby goes in and comes out a man. Many children who used to grow up in institutions are now in foster homes. Many children in institutions are not orphans. There are usually parents who visit; or if children are orphaned they are usually older; often siblings who do not want to be adopted or live with any other family. In some cases institutions are a better plan for a child than a foster home or an adoptive home. Older children have pasts, they often don't adjust well to another family situation. Children from deprived homes, children from homes where parents were drunk or drug addicts, often long to return to these homes; sometimes they run away from good foster homes and are found on the doorsteps of their own home."

"Do you find that there is a decrease in applicants for adopted children?"

"Yes, there has been a decrease in applicants and an increase in babies. This has enabled us to be more flexible in our requirements and regulations."

"Why do you think there is this trend?"

"First, there has been a lot done in the fertility field, so that more couples are able to have their own children. Second, we are now being approached by people who belong to the less numerous Depression generation and at the same time we are placing babies who are a product of the war boom."

"Do you have any follow up of children after they are placed?"

"Very little, except when the couple comes in to adopt a second or third child."

"Do you charge a placement fee?"

"Yes, we charge eleven and a half percent of the annual income when the first child is placed, eight percent when the second child is placed, and six and a half percent when the third child is placed. We have a very low endowment, which necessitates these high fees. This is unfortunate, since it keeps some people away from this agency."

"Do you require that a couple be married a certain length of time before you will accept their application?"

"Yes, they must have been married three years. We also require that they wait two years before they apply for a second child. These requirements have been constantly criticized by our prospective parents, who feel they are too rigid and unreasonable. Perhaps if we have more babies and the number of applicants does not increase we will make these rules more flexible."

"What are some of the reasons why couples are rejected?"

"Often one parent wants to adopt and the other one really does not want to or has great reservations—more often than not it is the woman who wants to adopt and the man who does not. Often our caseworkers will discover that there are serious marital difficulties, sometimes people want to adopt just to try to solve their marital problems; sometimes the medical report is bad —once we had a couple apply where the woman was dying of cancer but didn't know it. When people have to be rejected we try to let them know at their first intake interview. Often we have pressure from members of the community who dispute our rejection of a couple. Of course we cannot let them know why the couple was rejected."

"Do parents have any recourse if the adoption does not work out?"

"Not once the adoption is legal. Adoptive parents have the same responsibility as any other parents. There are rare cases when we will take a child back or remove him from the home; we took back a baby recently where there was increasing evidence of serious mental deterioration. We will place another child with this family, but not right away. This is a time of mourning for them, just as if they had lost a child of their own. The emphasis of our placements is finding the best family for the child; the children are our prime concern. Private placements emphasize the wishes of the adoptive parents—if any thought is given at all to the placement. We had a case recently where a lawyer arranged for a mother to place her baby with a couple; the girl gave birth to twins and one of the twins was born with a harelip, and the adoptive couple would only take the 'good' baby, not the 'bad.' The lawyer allowed them to adopt the 'good' baby and brought the handicapped baby to this agency. This is only one of the many shocking abuses of private placement. When girls come to the agency after some attempts to place their baby privately, they usually express great relief that they are able to work out a responsible plan for their child."

"How do you select a particular family for a particular child?"

"We try to estimate the capacity of the natural mother, her potential, temperament, and so on. Our rule of thumb in placement is 'a reciprocity of needs.' An intelligent child needs a home which offers stimulation, intelligent parents need a child who will respond to and benefit from the opportunities, educational and cultural, that they want for their children. Often, however, intelligent people push their children too hard. We placed a child of what we thought was a quite average mother with a quite average family. When they applied for a second child we tested the first child and she tested extremely well. We wondered whether we had not 'underplaced' this child, but when we interviewed the parents and observed them with the child we realized that though the child was more intelligent than the parents, the home was such that a child was encouraged to develop his own potential and a very bright child could develop beautifully with these parents, who did not expect their child to be mirror images of themselves."

Intelligent questions—intelligently answered! One wishes that the agency could broaden the scope of its activities to the extent of accepting other than "Catholic" babies. I would be quite willing to have little non-Catholic babies placed in good and loving Catholic homes through this agency. I will go still further. I would gladly see the orphaned children all baptized as Catholics if it meant they could find love and family.

It is only fair that we now take a good Jewish adoption agency as a sample of others like it. Such an agency may be found in several places, but one in New York City was chosen. It is a liberal agency, one that has eliminated many of the old delaying techniques. For example, a child is placed in the adoptive home within three to six months. There is no income requirement except the assurance that the family can support another child. There is no age limit for adoptive parents. The only question to be answered is whether these parents are the right ones for this child. Some agencies insist that the wife give up her job if she has one when the baby is placed. This agency asks only that she make a good arrangement for the baby's care, reasoning that if she had a child by birth, she would continue her job after having so planned. It is not required that the family own its home or even have a certain number of rooms. All that is asked is that there be room for the baby. Families who already have children are allowed to adopt. This agency has excellent social workers and does a careful job of selection, usually, of course, within the limitations of the Jewish faith. That it is able to do this and maintain such liberal standards makes it an example of what can be done to bring parents and child together when requirements, though functional, are simple enough to eliminate red tape.

Since New York is in process of changing its system of adoption from surrogates to the family court, thus unifying all services for children in the latter, it was interesting to discover that this agency is in favor of a unified family court instead of having separation and divorce in one court, support in another, adoption in still another, etc. The Catholic agency, it seems, was opposed to the unified court because it did not want separation and divorce to be transferred from the supreme court to the family court, which they felt is more psychiatrically oriented and would make divorce easier. A compromise was finally agreed upon, providing that a unified family court be established, handling all family matters except separation and divorce, which would be handled by the supreme court, unless that court recommended that a particular case be transferred to the family court. The unified family court was established two years ago, by the way, but it still lacks sufficient funds and staff. It will take time to set up the mechanism to handle adoption, since these are requiring that adoptions take place in the county of the adopting parents, and so on. It was decided to give concurrent jurisdictions over adoption to the surrogates' court and the family court for a two-year transitional period, until September, 1964, the family court to take over adoption completely at that time. The surrogates were not happy to turn over adoption to the family court, or so I was told. For a number of reasons they like this work and felt that they were doing a good job. A bill was introduced to keep adoption under concurrent jurisdiction for an indefinite period; the bill was passed by both houses, but the agencies were up in arms and enough pressure was put upon Governor Rockefeller by the social agencies so that he vetoed the bill. Unless the bill is reintroduced and goes through, the family court will take over in September of 1964. It is interesting that although the agencies are so ardent in their support of the family court and although they can now choose their forum for adoption cases, they almost always still use the surrogates' court rather than the family court. At first thought the unified family court seems a good idea. It is a new court, however, and therefore not predictable. Also like any other good idea, it must be implemented with minds, bodies and money in order to give it meaning.

In New York State there are two kinds of legal adoption: placement through an agency licensed by the State Department of Welfare, and placement by the natural mother. In New York—as in some other states —it is legally required in a private placement that the natural mother herself relinquish the child to the adoptive parents. In some courts the surrogate will put through the adoption, even though the adoptive parents have not met the natural mother, but in doing this the surrogate is a law unto himself. In New York City one third of adopted children go to relatives, one third are agency adoptions and one third are gray market, or privately placed.

Questions and answers with the Jewish agency went on:

"Does the agency ever place a child across religious lines?"

"Yes, there are three groups of children whom we will place across religious lines; first, children whose mothers are non-Jewish, but who ask that their child be placed with a Jewish family. Often in such cases the father is Jewish; in other cases the mother has heard that Jewish families are very close-knit and this appeals to her. Second, interracial children, usually Negro and white, are placed in Negro homes. Surrogates often will agree that to hold up an adoption of a Negro child for religious reasons is unfair, since it is not probable that another home will be found for this child. An interesting aspect of this problem is that the city has a policy of designating religions to all abandoned children by a process of rationing: one, two, three—Catholic, Protestant, Jewish. Third, there are the children with serious medical problems. Here, too, the surrogates are more lenient in their interpretation of the 'religious protection' clause of the New York law. If the agency suggests that the child be placed in a family of a religion different from that of the child's natural mother, the court will usually rule that placement along the religious lines is not practicable in this instance."

"Can a couple of different religions adopt a child through your agency?"

"Yes, if they agree to follow the Jewish religion in their home and bring up their children in the Jewish faith."

"What qualifications has the agency established for adoptive parents?"

"Years ago the philosophy of the agency was based on finding a child for a family, now the philosophy is finding a family for a child. The requirements are much more lenient. There are more children available and fewer applications from would-be adoptive parents. The agency no longer tries to match physical features of the parents and the child, and they are more lenient as to the age limit of the parents. Also there are older children available for older parents."

"Will the agency place a child in a home where there is already a natural child?"

"We prefer not to—they feel that it is better for the child to be raised with other adopted children. Such restrictions are waived, however, if the couples are interested in adopting children who are difficult to place, that is, nonwhite, older, handicapped."

"How old are most of the infants when you place them?"

"About three months old. Babies are rarely placed from the hospital, because the agency feels that a mother is not ready to decide whether she wishes to place her child for adoption until the child is born. Before the babies are placed for adoption they are examined in the agency clinic and then cared for in licensed boarding homes in the suburbs. The agency feels that it is very helpful, in selecting the right home for the baby, to have this period of observation."

"Do you have shelters for unwed mothers?"

"Yes, we operate several residences for unmarried mothers. These are the only residences in the United States for unwed Jewish mothers."

"How long do you usually know a couple before you place a child with them?"

"Generally it is ten to fifteen months between the initial inquiry and the date of placement."

"Do you find that there are many children who are 'not adoptable'?"

"No, there are very few."

"How old are the children who are placed?"

"Children are accepted up to two years of age, possibly three years old. If children are not placed by this time they are sent to another institution. But most are placed by the time they are three years old, only two or three a year are not."

"Do you think that the fact that children can usually only be placed in homes of their own religion keeps many children from being placed, and necessitates the children's remaining in institutions?"

Here several persons in the agency speak to this point. First of all they want to make clear that religion rarely keeps any child from being placed; that with Catholics, for example, as with other groups, there were many more childless couples wanting children than there are babies who need homes. They then go on to say that institutions are not the evil places that they are thought to be. For some children institutional life is a better plan than family life in an adoptive home. This is especially true of large families, sisters and brothers, where it is better to keep them together as a family group; older children, who remember well their own families and do not wish to be adopted by another family. Also, most children in these institutions are not orphans. Many have one or two parents, who perhaps cannot support them for a while, or who have marital problems and feel that the children would be better off outside the home until these are resolved; some parents are ill, but visit children regularly and have strong relationships with them; often, a mother dies and the father must work, cannot care for children at home, etc. In other words, there is a real need for these institutions. Children here are not abandoned. Usually they are in institutions because it is felt that this is a better plan for them than temporary foster care in a family situation. For those children who are difficult to place but need family life while they await placement, the agency has an increasing number of foster homes.

I listen and take up my questions again.

"If the adoption does not work out, do the adoptive parents have any recourse?"

"The parents have one year in which to change their minds, from the time of placement to the time of the legal adoption. After this they are parents and assume the same responsibility as any other parents."

"Do you have any requirements for adoptive parents besides religious requirements?"

"They must have been married for at least three years. We feel this is a necessary requirement to ascertain that the marriage is a sound one, and to make sure that the couple have sought enough medical advice to be pretty certain that they cannot have their own children."

"Do you limit the number of children you will place with a family?"

"No, we have placed as many as six children with one family."

"Does each child have to have his own room?"

"No, we only require that each child have his own bed!"

This is an unusual agency, I conclude when we part. It puts the child first and it moves toward adoption with careful speed. The people in the agency do not think that the child is better off under their foster care plan than it is in an adoptive family. Any adoptive family, if it is loving and accepting, is infinitely better than the best of foster care.

The next agency to be sampled is a Protestant agency. It has high repute and in many aspects deserves it. It is the favorite charity of wealthy young society women. The buildings and equipment are what every agency longs for and they have a fine staff of highly trained social workers. I know this agency of old, for some years ago it gave a child of mixed race to Welcome House. As it happened, I was the first one to see this child, for I was visiting the agency when they told us they wished to refer the child to Welcome House because at that time they found it difficult to place children of mixed race. Since then, I must interject in all fairness, they have made remarkable progress in this regard. But the little boy, when I saw him, showed definite signs of malnutrition. I have seen thousands of such children in India and China, and I know the heartbreaking symptoms. I exclaimed at his condition and was immediately corrected by the very poised young social worker.

"It is quite impossible that any of our children are undernourished," she told me. "We have an excellent dietician."

This was true. They did have such a person, and as she explained to me, she gave careful diet directions to every foster mother. As it happened, however, the foster mother of this little boy was Italian and she did not read the diet list. Perhaps she could not. At any rate, the little boy was fed improperly. When Welcome House took custody he was immediately sent to the Children's Hospital, and it was found that he was suffering from lead poisoning. His diet lacked essential ingredients and he was chewing painted wood, the side of his crib, his toys, the arms of chairs, the edges of tables, in an instinctive effort to get the needed minerals. We saved him, but it was several years before his spindly legs grew sturdy and his potbelly disappeared. Every intention was good in this fine agency, but there was no special eye watching over the child, the eye of love and concern.

On my recent visit the executive director of this same agency began by saying that she felt that hers was a particularly good agency because they handled not only adoption but all aspects of family service.

"Do you have an opportunity, because of this, to observe the adopted child after the legal adoption?"

"Yes, as a matter of fact the adoptive parents come to the service with their problems more readily than the natural parents."

"Do you find that adopted children are particularly troubled about being adopted at certain ages?"

"Yes, between the ages of seven and eight, and then again in adolescence."

"Is there any difference in the reaction of boys and girls?"

"Yes, boys seem to have a tougher 'row to hoe' between seven and eight, when they are learning to read and gaining a sense of their own identity. Girls have a harder time during adolescence. With girls who have been placed badly, many think of themselves as potential unwed mothers. We find that many of our unwed mothers were adopted. Usually they were adopted privately, or a natural child followed, or there was discord in the marriage of their adoptive parents."

"How many children will you place with a family?"

"Usually the maximum is two."

"Will you place an adopted child where there is already a natural child?"

"Yes, but then we prefer to place two children; we feel it is better for the adopted child to grow up with another child who is also adopted. We rarely place a child where parents have more than one natural or adopted child because we feel that there are too many childless couples who want children."

"Do you place any older children?"

"Yes, usually those are between the ages of one and three years old. They are almost always of preschool age."

"How long must a couple wait after they have adopted a child to apply for another?"

"We feel there should be a minimum age difference of two years between children."

"Does a couple have to be married for a certain length of time before they can apply?"

"Yes, they have to have been married at least five years, on the theory that neither the stability of the marriage nor sterility have had time to be established before this."

"Is there an age limit for adoptive parents?"

"Couples under twenty-five will only be considered if definite organic reasons for sterility have been verified. Usually we will not place an infant with a couple where the wife is over forty or the husband is over forty-five. Exceptions are made, however, if we feel that a child would be better placed with older parents."

"Would you place a Negro child with a white family or vice versa?"

"Children are generally placed in families of their own race. In cases of mixed racial backgrounds, placement is made with parents whose own characteristics most closely approximate the child's. The only time we would place a partially Negro child with a white family is if the child is white—that is, if an anthropologist and physician examined the baby and found no Negroid characteristics such as a thick neck, 'blue spots', etc. Even in this case we would of course tell the adoptive parents of the child's parentage."

"Do you find that parents have many specific requests as to the child they want?"

"Most parents want a child as much like themselves as possible. We have found, however, that more couples request girls than boys. This seems perplexing, as we know that most natural parents, if they have any preference, desire a boy first, or at least the father desires a son first."

Another private, nonsectarian agency in another state answered also in general terms.

"How old are the majority of the children at the time you place them?"

"Most of them are under three months old, although we have placed children up to three years old. We would never accept the surrender of a child by the mother until the baby is born. Before adoption, babies are placed in boarding homes. We emphasize the development of boarding homes, which will accept older babies, and the development of Negro boarding homes, which will keep babies the longer time it may require to find adoptive homes for them. Some boarding homes are potential adoptive homes when the baby becomes legally available for adoption."

"Would you place a child where there is already a natural child?"

"Yes, we would and have."

"Do you limit the number of children you will place with one family?"

"No, we have placed as many as three children with one family."

"Would you place a Negro child with white parents or a white child with Negro parents?"

Two social workers, who were both Negroes, were asked to speak on this question. "This is a problem of our society and it is too easy to pinpoint it in adoption. White parents simply do not want to adopt Negro or Puerto Rican children at this stage in our country's development, and Negroes, too, want children as much like themselves as possible. White families will more often adopt Oriental children or American-Indian children, particularly white couples from the East, where prejudice against these minorities is not strong. We have participated in the Child Welfare League project to try to find homes for American-Indian children."

"Would you place a child across religious lines? The religious problem is a political one."

"By New York State law we are compelled, insofar as it is practicable, to place a baby in a home of its own religious faith."

"Do you place Catholic or Jewish children, too?"

"We recently agreed to turn over Jewish children to a Jewish agency, since they have more choice of parents for the few Jewish children who come in here. We will initiate a study of Catholic couples in proportion to the Catholic babies we have in our care. Most Catholic babies go to Catholic agencies."

"Do you make any effort to meet the father of the babies? Is any responsibility placed on him?"

"No, we do not make any efforts to meet the father —the girls don't want this—although we would of course be glad to meet him."

"Do you charge a placement fee?"

"Yes, and our fees are on a sliding scale; the maximum is twelve hundred and fifty dollars for couples earning over sixteen thousand dollars a year. We waive or adjust contributions from couples, particularly Negro couples, when we feel this will facilitate their ability to provide a home for the child."

"How long do you know most couples before you place a child with them?"

"Usually from six months to one year."

"Does the adoptive family have any recourse if the adoption does not work out?"

"Yes, the agency will take the child back in such cases; they feel it is better for the child and the family."

"How do you select a particular baby for a particular home?"

"Our emphasis is the reverse. We select homes for babies. We do consider, however, the values of the parents, what they want in a child. Some parents want a child whose parents were college graduates, some want a child of a particular nationality, some want a child who will look like themselves. Some parents do not care about the heredity of the baby, others have very strong feelings. What people want in a child is often irrational. The majority want a child most like what they think they are; how they see themselves is therefore a crucial factor to determine."

"How much do you tell the adoptive parents about the natural parents?"

"As much as we think they want to know, with the exception of identifiable information. We feel that the adoptive parents have to accept not only the child but also the child's parents if the adoption is to be successful. They must not feel superior to the child's natural parents or this will manifest itself in their attitude to the child."

"What happens to the children who are not easily adoptable?"

"In August, 1962, we undertook a five-year demonstration program to provide foster homes for children in well-baby hospital wards and temporary shelters of the city. These are children of racial minorities or physically handicapped, who are not easy to place.

The long-term foster-care project was underwritten by special foundation grants. Foster parents receive two dollars a day for the care of these children. These children will remain under our protection until they reach eighteen years of age."

"Do you have a shelter for unwed mothers?"

"No, we do not have a shelter yet. We make arrangements for them in small hotels. We provide counseling and casework services for them before and after the birth of their babies. To many we provide financial assistance to help with their maternity expenses and hospital bills, and also to help them afterward until they find a job, et cetera."

"How old are most of these women?"

"Over half are in the sixteen- to twenty-four-year age group; the next largest group is between the ages of twenty-five and thirty. Our experience does *not* support the opinion commonly held that the number of unmarried mothers fifteen years of age or younger is increasing."

"Are these women mostly from one socio-economic group? Or are they fairly well distributed over the whole of society?"

"They are fairly well distributed, mostly average working girls, high school students, et cetera. Some are college girls, some are women who are married but separated from their husbands."

"Are natural mothers told about the family with whom their child is placed?"

"Yes, they are told quite a bit about the family. If the child is handicapped they follow the child's welfare until the child is placed. Natural mothers are usually very interested in the plans that are made for their child."

There are many excellent agencies existing for the care and custody of children. I have given an example of the Catholic agency which is concerned about children of that faith; a Jewish agency primarily concerned about Jewish children, but which does not eliminate others; and a Protestant agency. The Catholic agency is not unique in its policy of giving children only to parents of that religion. The Lutheran faith, although Protestant, limits adoption of their children to Lutheran families, and there are scattered cases of such agencies in other Protestant branches.

Perhaps the most satisfying agency studied was a private, nonsectarian community adoption agency. In answer to this question of sectarianism, the reply was that children are placed with adoptive parents of the same faith as the natural parents if this is possible, but only if it is possible. They are not kept unadopted for religious reason.

This is an agency in New York State, where child welfare agencies have developed historically along religious lines. They are primarily financed by religious federations rather than by a community chest or some other nonsectarian fund-raising body. Nevertheless, these agencies are the most inflexible in the country in many ways. In the Midwest, however, the adoption picture is far more progressive. Cleveland has probably the most advanced adoption program. The sectarian agencies in Cleveland are part of a community chest which has a rotating board, hence new ideas are constantly explored and different people have an opportunity to make decisions. The progressive attitude is expressed in the fact that the board members of the community chest and the professionals (social workers, etc.) are partners. In New York, too, the situation is unusual, because adoptions are under the jurisdiction of the surrogates' court, a "political outfit with patronage." As mentioned elsewhere, in September of 1964 the jurisdiction was transferred to the family court.

Questions and answers with the private, nonsectarian community agency mentioned above went like this, in effect:

"Do you ever make interracial placements?" I asked.

"Yes."

"Do you place Negro children with white families?"

"Yes, but these are special kinds of families, whose way of life lends itself to such a thing, that is, missionaries, theatrical people, ministers. The most difficult problem is the Negro children. Negro parents who are interested in adoption are very concerned about the shade of the child. They desire only a child of their coloring, or a child who is lighter than they."

"Is this a nonsectarian agency?"

"Yes—but the only way we can be nonsectarian in New York with its religious protection law is to adhere very strictly to religious lines."

"Do you meet the natural mothers of the babies you place?"

"Yes."

"What is their average age?"

"Most of the unwed mothers are from eighteen to twenty-five."

"Are these women from one particular class or are they fairly well distributed over all of society?"

"No, not in this agency. We get mostly persons of low income."

"Do you charge a placement fee?"

"Yes, and our fees are on a sliding scale: a thousand dollars, maximum; fifty dollars, minimum."

"How long do you usually know a couple before you accept them?"

"About three months."

"Do you place any abandoned children here?"

"Yes, we get some of the Protestant children, or those who are designated Protestant."

"Are there many adoptable children who are not getting placed?"

"Yes, but these are mostly older children, nonwhite children or children who are handicapped emotionally or psychologically. Ours is a state-wide agency. Children in our care come to us from all areas of New York State. They range in age from infancy to about ten years old. The couples who come to us are also from all areas of New York State. This differentiates us from other agencies in the city, which are mainly local."

VI

And Yet They Fail

Wherein then do these agencies, excellent in themselves and typical of many others, fail? For fail they
do to a marked degree, since so many children still
remain in orphanages and in foster care. We cannot
be satisfied with the foster home as a substitute for the
permanency of, first, the child's natural family, and
then, if that proves impossible, the adoptive. Failure
still lies mainly, I believe, in the lack of co-ordination
between all agencies in the community, state and nation, so that although there is duplication in staff, effort
and cost, the goal is not attained. What is the goal? It

is to give every lost child a permanent home and family. It is to empty every orphanage of little children, who now linger on and on, indefinitely, and place them for adoption, or failing adoption, in foster homes. Especially, it is to find the babies now lost in hospitals because no one wants them.

Last year there were hundreds of babies living in cribs in New York hospitals because there was no place for them to go. Most of them had been there nearly a year, some had been there for almost two years. They were deserted by the women who bore them, their natural mothers. But they were also deserted by the community. They were unwanted children. Yes, I know that in some countries they would not have been allowed to live, especially the girls. I suppose it is better to live in a hospital than to die at birth—I do not know.

One of these hospitals, for example, serves as a children's shelter, a refuge for well babies who are abandoned. Three hundred deserted children live there. It is the only home they know. Still, it is a hospital, a quiet, well-scrubbed hospital. The first thing that one notices, that one feels, on entering, is the quiet. These babies do not cry. They have learned that crying brings no results. No one has time, they know. If someone comes it is one of the many who come, the many strange faces. But there is a sound, a regular mechanical beat. It comes from a metal box that transmits seventy-two pulse beats a minute. This sound beats through the rooms in a steady rhythm, simulating the beat of the mother's heart before the baby is born. The babies lie in their cribs listening, continuing the life of the unborn. Yes, though they are separated from their mothers and from the warm human womb, which provided the early shelter for growth, they are unborn but no longer sheltered and secure. When I think of them, lying in their cribs listening to the mechanical heartbeat, I am moved to anger and tears. I can allow myself neither. There are too many such children.

At another hospital not far away there are still more children, deserted by their mothers, their families, their communities. They are confined in the prison of their cribs, and to comfort themselves and to have something to do, they rock back and forth. They play with their own hands, caressing them as though they belonged to someone else, because they have no other hands than their own to hold and to caress. Most of them never smile. Neither do they talk or walk. They have never been outdoors. But they do not cry or protest, for they know nothing else. They think this is the way of life, and perhaps they are right. Perhaps for them this is the way life is. Take one of them up from its crib, any one of them, and you feel a dead weight in your arms. There is no response. They have never seen a familiar face, and so, no faces are strange to them. They are accustomed. They will not respond to your friendly face, for they see many friendly faces, but never the special face of the one. There are hundreds of faces in this hospital. Thirty professionals, four hundred and eighty-two employes and three hundred voluntary aides these children see at one time or another, but among them is not the special face of the one. Sometimes four babies are spoon-fed by one too-busy nurse. But she does not belong to any of them, either, and they know it. Did I say these are well babies? But even well babies, if they stay in their cribs too long, become ill. Their skin begins to scale, and then it is cut by the rough sheets.

Forty thousand unadoptable children in our country! How does it come about? Some private adoption agencies will not allow a child to be adopted until his runaway mother is found. But many such mothers cannot be found. So the child is kept an orphan. In desperation a campaign was once set up to find parents, either adoptive or foster parents. It was a crash program, well carried on at the time, in part on television and through newspapers. The response was good. It is always encouraging to discover in a community that there is such response when there is leadership. But there was not enough. There are still seven thousand children in the city of New York alone who need to find the loving care that can come only from family life. The mechanical heart must be replaced by a human heart.

I remember a baby that was brought into my own home from a crib in a hospital. Danny was his name. He was ten months old. He could not sit up, nor could he creep. He made no effort to move. He did not know what a toy was, nor did he make a sound. He was silent, his large dark eyes blank. I had been asked to keep him for a while to see whether he could develop. An adoptive home waited for him if he showed sufficient ability to develop. The change was miraculous. In a few days he seemed to understand that he was living in a family with people who loved him and played with him and talked to him. In a month he was creeping and making sounds of baby talk, and in a few more days he was pulling himself to his feet. In two months he was almost up to his age level, and ready to go to his adoptive family. They had visited him meanwhile, so that when he went with them, they were not strangers.

What would have happened to Danny if no one had found him? I do not know. I suppose no one knows.

But as one mother said, when she was given a hospital baby:

"She was six months old when she came to me, but coming from a hospital, she hadn't learned to do the normal things that a six-month-old would do because, although she had perfectly good care, she didn't have the love that home life gives. There is a difference. I found that out. There was a time when I didn't know this, but I know it now. You get a baby that is a well baby, she's . . . she has no medical problems, but she's sick in certain other ways. For instance, this baby came to me and I couldn't pick her up for almost three months after I got her because she was afraid of being held. I learned—I taught her to let me pick her up by walking into the room and saying, 'I'm coming,' and playing with her when I got there, touching her, rubbing her hands, and as time passed she began to respond, and now she is really a very loving little girl. She enjoys being held. She's very affectionate, but she had to be taught. She had love and she had affection in the hospital, but it was fleeting. In the middle of the night I could go to her if she cried, and I could pat her, and I had time to do it. But you would have to think, in the hospital the nurse would have more than one baby to care for and she would have to spread herself out and pat a lot of them, and she could make it maybe one minute. I could hold her as long as she needed. Home life makes a big difference."

There is a difference indeed. It is the difference between death and life. And the goal is: no more lost children.

No more lost children? A child can be lost though he is fed and sheltered and sent to school. A child is lost if there is no human being with whom he can communicate in terms of love, a human being to whom he can turn as a flower turns to the sun, a human being who is the center of his life, and in the center of whose life he is. That center must be in the family and that family must be in a community. The relationship of the child to his family is the same as the family should have to the community. They are members one of another.

Our whole social structure is trembling under the shocks of change. Our experiments have been made for us, under Communism. Even before Castro, in Cuba many unwanted babies were deposited in the *crèches* of religious organizations. What were these *crèches*? They were cradles set in revolving doors, the entrance to orphanages. Any woman could put her baby in the cradle and leave, unannounced, unknown. The baby, nameless, was taken into the orphanage and reared. Fed and clothed but without individual love and family care, the child's emotional life never developed. Trained in routine behavior and homeless group life, he became easy prey for the dictator.

Or take the case of China. In pre-Communist China the family was the central unit of society, its controlling element, its refuge for the lonely child and the lonely aged. But the Communists, seizing power, became jealous of the strong family ties and sought to destroy the family by taking the child and putting him with other children, away from parents and kin. The Communists took away the old and put them into hostels ironically called Happiness Halls. Ironically, because, separated from their families, the old faded quickly into death, and death has swept into oblivion many, many children, who died in numbers that frightened even the Communists and forced them to relent to the extent of establishing families again to replace the communes. Nature is strong. When the natural tie between parents and children is broken, adoption must take its place. Adoption, as old in history as the human family, is the only alternative for the protection of the lost child and for the satisfaction of the childless couple. The family, natural or adoptive, is the living link between those past and the future.

And Yet They Fail

The family is the continuity of mankind. *It is the responsibility of the community to see that the continuity continues.*

What is the community? Properly speaking, for the child—the neglected child, the homeless child, the orphan—there are several communities. First of all there is the national community. The federal government evinces a general concern for children. There is also some co-operation between the federal bureaus and state and private agencies. An example of this is a program now in progress, in which the Child Welfare League, the United Bureau of Indian Affairs and several private agencies are working together to find adoptive homes for American-Indian children. In Pennsylvania new adoption laws are in preparation which, when passed, will fix the termination of parental rights and responsibilities, and free a child for adoption. This pending legislation will follow the recommendations of the United States Children's Bureau. Another such co-operative effort is one mutually sponsored by the Child Welfare League and the Children's Bureau. It is a cost analysis of adoption proceedings in order to find out exactly how much it costs, or should cost, to place a child in an adoptive home. It is hoped that such a study will reduce costs and standardize adoption proceedings in financial terms.

The growing amount of co-operation between the states themselves is a heartening sign of increasing efficiency in finding adoptive homes, especially for nonwhite children, where the need is the greatest. In New Jersey, for example, an advisory interracial committee is working closely with the Urban League in rousing interest on the part of local communities for finding homes. In New York City, nearby, the Department of Welfare provides the greater part of the funds for private agencies to care for children and if possible to place them for adoption, most of them nonwhite.

There is beginning to be a very successful adoption exchange, too, between the states. Each co-operating state department lists all the available children in one region, and the available homes. These lists circulate and make possible the placement of children who will fare better if they are placed at a distance from their natural parents, and provide a wider opportunity for other children to find good adoptive homes.

If there is more co-operation between the states in the area of child adoption, there remain also many differences. The Children's Bureau in the Department of Health, Education and Welfare in Washington has published a guide for the states in revising their adoption laws. One of the suggestions is that it be made illegal for any unauthorized agency or private individual to act as an intermediary in adoptions, whether paid or voluntary. The states have accepted this in various ways. To date, Alabama, California, Connecticut, Delaware, Illinois, Maryland, Massachusetts, Michigan, Nevada, New York, North Carolina, Ohio, Oregon, Rhode Island, South Dakota, Tennessee, Texas, Utah and Washington, D.C., have decreed that children can only be placed for adoption by licensed agencies or persons holding licenses. The other states continue as they have.

States vary, too, in the matter of receiving fees for adoption; in fact, some states have laws prohibiting the charging of fees for child placement. Practically speaking, such laws mean that adoptions are restricted to public agencies, for private agencies cannot exist unless they ask fees to cover their costs. Charity proves to be inadequate. The states which have passed laws against fees are Colorado, except as approved by the court; and against legal fees, Arizona, Texas and Washington, D.C. In the District of Columbia the law was changed in 1954 to allow a licensed child-placing agency, operating only for religious or charitable purposes, to charge fees amounting to cost if no part of such earnings accrues to any shareholders or individuals.

Religion, always a divisive force, continues to be so in the area of adoption, in spite of all statements to the contrary. In California, for example, while there is no specific mention of religion in the laws, the practice is nevertheless that religious faith is discussed with the natural parents before adoption is completed. In Connecticut, while there is no mention of religion in the laws, the practice is nevertheless that children are placed in homes where the religion is that of the natural parent. Nebraska, although it has no legal religious restrictions on adoptions, does as a matter of policy place children in homes of like religious faith, where it is possible. Some states have incorporated into law that children be placed in homes where the religion is that of the natural parents, if practicable. Delaware allows the mother to sign a waiver, and Pennsylvania specifies that religion is not to be a bar to adoption. Massachusetts, Missouri, Oregon, Rhode Island, South Dakota and Washington, D.C., make it clear that the religion of the natural parents is to be continued in the adoptive family, if at all possible. How possible or impossible it is depends very largely on prejudices of the social worker and the judge.

There are other interesting variations in the religious outlook in relation to adoption. Michigan's law reads that the suitability of the adoption of this child by that petitioner shall take into account racial, religious and cultural background. New Hampshire law provides that due regard shall be given to the race and religion of the child and the petitioner. The New Hampshire State Board of Child Welfare insists that every reasonable effort be made in selecting a family home or an institution of the same religious faith as the natural parent or parents of the child. The New Mexico Department of Welfare has no laws pertaining to religious restriction in the placement of children but the religious preference of the natural mother is usually followed although mothers often give permission to have their children placed in the home of any religion so that it can be done as quickly as possible. In Ohio there are no religious restrictions in the statutes themselves. However, the Department of Welfare rules for agencies and boarding homes state that a child shall be placed in a foster home that can provide him with an opportunity for spiritual development which does not conflict with the broad religious preference of his parents. Thus an agency should not place a child in a home of a religious faith other than the one preferred by the parents or sole parent, or if the child is old enough to have established a meaningful relationship with a religious organization, in a home different from that religion. The other states make no mention of religion in their laws, but practice varies with the inclinations prevailing among agencies and judges. In Louisiana, however, it is required that the adopting parents be of the same religion as the natural ones.

It is interesting to discover that racial restrictions, though practiced in all the Southern states and probably in many of the Northern states, are not mentioned in the laws, except that race is one of the factors to be considered in determining the suitability of an adoption. An exception is in Kentucky, where the law specifies: "Whenever within a five-year period after an adoption is finalized a child reveals traits of ethnological ancestry different from those of the adoptive parents and of which the adoptive parents had no knowledge or information prior to the adoption, the adoption can be annulled."

South Carolina has its own form of racial restriction: "No person in this state shall adopt an illegitimate child unless the father and mother of such child if both were unmarried at the time of its birth could have lawfully contracted matrimony under the constitution and laws of this state."

Texas declares: "No white child can be adopted by a

Negro person nor can a Negro child be adopted by a white person."

In Missouri the laws says: "An adoption may be set aside within five years when a person shall prove to be a member of a race, the members of which are prohibited by the laws of this state from marriage with members of the race to which the parents by adoption belong."

There is a wide variation among the states in laws governing inheritance. Most states wish to end the relationship between the child and the natural parents and set up a legal parent-child relationship between the child and the adoptive parents, but several states permit the adopted child to inherit from its natural as well as from its adoptive parents, and from blood relatives as well as adoptive relatives, creating, I should think, an ambivalence. Alabama varies this by stating that an adopted child cannot inherit from natural parents unless it is so specified in the final decree of adoption. In Florida an adopted child may inherit from its natural parents; in Georgia adoptive parents can only inherit that which the adopted child acquires after the final order of adoption, and they cannot inherit what the child has acquired or inherited from blood relatives. Indiana maintains that the adopted child can inherit from his blood relatives or other kin, and Maine, too, decrees that the adopted child shall not lose his right to inherit from his natural parents or kindred. Massachusetts allows an adopted child to inherit from both the adoptive and the natural parents, while in Louisiana the adopted child continues as the lawful heir of natural parents. Michigan says that an adopted child is not debarred from inheriting from or through his natural parents. The same is true of the adopted child in Utah, but he is not held to be "issue" of adoptive parent. Texas declares that natural parents and kin cannot inherit from the child, but the adopted child shall inherit from its natural parents. In Vermont the adopted child may inherit from natural parents, although natural parents may not inherit from the child. In Ohio and Missouri the law provides that although the adopted child may inherit from adoptive parents and their kin, he may not inherit property left to "heirs of the body" of his adoptive parents.

One important aspect of law in regard to adoption is that of termination of the right of natural parents, freeing a child for adoption. I have already discussed New York in this regard, but many other states have also provided judicially for termination of parental rights upon abandonment, neglect, cruelty, depravity or long-time prison sentences. Such is the case with

Alabama, Alaska, Arizona, California, Connecticut, Hawaii, Idaho, Indiana, Iowa, Kentucky, Massachusetts, North Carolina, North Dakota, Ohio, Oklahoma, Pennsylvania, Rhode Island, South Dakota, Texas, Utah, Vermont, Washington, West Virginia and Wyoming. The remaining states allow for termination of parental rights if the court decides this is in the best interests of the child. Again much depends on the passions and prejudices of the social worker and the judge.

A strange contradiction appears in some states in regard to annulment of adoption. Although our general laws of adoption declare that an adoptive child shall be in all respects considered as a natural child, this is denied in Minnesota, Utah, Missouri, Georgia and Iowa, where after five to seven years an adoption may be annulled if the child develops feeblemindedness, epilepsy or venereal disease as a result of conditions prior to the adoption or unknown to the adoptive parents. California has the same provisions, omitting venereal diseases. Delaware and Florida say that after two years adoption cannot be annulled. Hawaii permits none after one year. Kentucky provides that after the expiration of two years from the adoption decree, its validity cannot be attacked by reason of any irregularity in procedures. Maine provides (as of 1959) that any judge or probate may, on petition of two or more persons, for good causes shown, reverse and annul an adoption decree. Mississippi provides that no action shall be brought to set aside any final decree of adoption except within six months of the entry thereof. Nebraska provides that the adoption is valid unless action is brought within two years. North Dakota provides that proceedings to attack an adoption must commence within one year from date of entering the decree of adoption. Washington, D.C., provides that an adoption decree cannot be invalidated unless the attack is filed within one year following the time the final decree became effective.

New York is unique in its laws concerning the abrogation of an adoption. It provides for abrogation by mutual consent or abrogation by or on behalf of the adopted child on grounds of cruelty, misuse, inability or refusal to support, maintain or educate, an attempt to change or the actual making of a change, or the failure to safeguard the religion of such child, or any other violation of duty on the part of the adoptive parent toward such child. An adoptive parent who has adopted through an authorized agency may also apply to a judge or surrogate for abrogation of an adoption because of the wilfull desertion of the adoptive parents by the adopted child, or because of any misdemeanor or ill behavior of the child. If the judge determines on proof that the adopted child has violated his duty toward his adoptive parent and that due regard to the interests of both requires that such adoption be abrogated, an order shall be made and entered accordingly.

There are, in addition to the above, certain laws of special interest. In California, for example, a taxpayer may, when computing his income tax return, deduct expenses connected with the adoption of a child, including the medical and hospital expenses of the mother of an adopted child incident to the child's birth; any legal and other fees paid to a welfare agency; and costs relating to the adoption. These expenses must exceed three percent of the adjusted gross income, however, and the maximum deduction for a joint return is twenty-five hundred dollars; the maximum deduction for separate returns, twelve hundred dollars.

In Colorado, if the state is unable to provide any child with a family home through voluntary adoption within six months from the time of its commitment, then as far as possible and for the best interests of the child it shall be its duty to provide for boarding-out of said child in a suitable family home until he is adopted or shall have reached the age of sixteen years.

Minnesota has a special provision for college tuition for state wards. Children who are neglected or dependent on the Commissioner of Public Welfare are eligible for special consideration in the matter of tuition payments at the University of Minnesota, but not at state colleges. The University of Minnesota grants free tuition upon certification by the Commissioner of Public Welfare.

Finally, the length of the waiting period between the time the child is placed in the adoptive home and the issuance of the final decree varies from state to state. Usually it is either six months or a year, and usually it can be waived by the court.

So much for the federal and state community of the lonely child. While they influence his environment and therefore his life, both are as remote from him as the sun in the sky. What he knows is only his own town, his immediate community. What we must ask for his sake is whether this town, this local community, is providing for him the environment in which he can grow and develop to his full potential. Is the community concerned on his behalf? If not, then it fails him. Am I saying that the local community is responsible for every family within its area, for every child born within its confines? Yes, that is what I am saying. And unless this is true, our democracy fails. For democracy depends upon its citizens, and citizens are

only people and people are shaped by what happens
to them.

Our communities are rich in service organizations,
in voluntary agencies for charity and special diseases,
each pleading its case for public funds, each maintain-
ing offices and staffs. But they are seldom co-ordinated
in their efforts and the needy individual is lost in a
maze of red tape. For example in one city, near which
I live, there are twenty-seven organizations to help the
blind, yet only the other day a parent of two blind
girls, living in that same city, asked me where she
should go to get help. None of these many organizations, she said, were able to consider her daughters as
entities, in the totality of their personal need. A multi-
plicity of services and none really serving! As I said
earlier, every community needs a central co-operating
group of responsible citizens, combining government,
professional and lay persons, a small working-group,
dedicated and responsible, a group that seeks out the
needy and sees that their needs are attended to.

VII

The Child without a Country

My thoughts return again and again, however, to the child who has no community, no state, no nation. What of the world's children, many of them fathered by American men abroad? In Korea alone, as of the year 1961, there were some sixty-five thousand children living in orphanages and some twenty-five thousand homeless children wandering the streets. Most of the wandering children are boys, for girls are often taken into households to be brought up as servants. The Korean government plans to put these wandering children into institutions at the rate of five thousand a year but as of now no funds are available to pursue the plan. No agencies serve the wandering children, except that in Seoul the Salvation Army sometimes gives shelter for a night and provides an evening meal. In the Anglican church of the same city about seventy-five beggar boys find a place to sleep each night, get a bath and simple teaching in reading, writing and arithmetic. Clergymen and theological students try to find jobs for some of the boys.

Various agencies try to secure food and shelter for the wandering children and to help the orphanages. Of these I will not speak now, since they do not try to find adoptive homes for the children. I myself have visited typical orphanages in Korea and I can only say that the conditions are pitiable in spite of the valiant efforts of the Koreans, who have nothing to share with the children except poverty. I remember too many faces of eager intelligent children, doomed, it seems, to be lost, for jobs are scarce in Korea and can seldom, without education and family backing, be secured on any level. Of the handicapped and the maimed, what can be said save that they have no chance whatever except to become beggars? As I write these words I see a face that I try not to remember. It is the face of a boy of thirteen, in an orphanage near Seoul, a polio victim, whose only means of locomotion was wriggling on his stomach in the dust. He was barely able to lift his head a few inches, but it was enough for me to see an intelligent, beautiful face. What can one do except remember? Yet I think of another boy with polio, four years old, born in Japan, half-American, half-Japanese. He was as crippled as the beautiful boy in Korea, but we got him into the United States. It was difficult, all but impossible, for he was not the sort of immigrant we permit to enter our land of the free and home of the brave. At first we had to promise that he was a visitor. As a visitor he went into the home of a physician specializing in his particular handicap. As a visitor he underwent treatment and care and was given love. I saw him last when he was seven years old. He had not been able to walk when he came as a visitor, but now he ran to meet me. A light brace on one leg was all that he needed now, and his adoptive father said he would need nothing by the time he was fifteen.

"Have you problems?" I asked.

"No," the father replied. Then he added, "Well, yes, Tommy answers questions rather wildly in school. We don't understand it."

"What do you mean?" I asked.

"Well," the father said, "his teacher called up yesterday to say that Tommy insists that a dog has only two legs. He was supposed to say four when she asked him, of course. But he would not yield. When he came home I told him he was wrong. Still he wouldn't yield. He said the front two legs were not legs. Now, you know, that's odd."

I reflected. No, it was not odd. In Japan, the front two legs of a dog are not called legs but hands. I explained this to the American father and he burst into laughter and rushed to the telephone to tell the teacher that Tommy was neither odd nor stubborn. Ah me, there are a thousand stories to tell of these children. But the ones that cannot be told, or when they are told break the heart, are the stories of those half-American children who wander the streets of Korea and Okinawa, or have as their only shelter the overcrowded orphanages. I wonder how these thousands of orphans will affect the Asian society of tomorrow, these many, many children who will never know what a father is, or what a family can mean.

Can we be responsible for these half-American children? In a sense, I suppose we are more responsible than the people of other countries, and for two reasons: first, we are a mixed people and many of our citizens are Oriental, thus providing more potential adoptive families; second, an unknown number of these children are fathered by Americans living and working abroad as military and other personnel. How many such half-American children exist cannot be known. In Korea a girl or woman who has a child out of wedlock is considered a prostitute, and she tends to keep her child, if a girl, as decoy for American servicemen. It is inevitable that most of these mixed-race children will never leave the country where they were born. In such cases, agencies must see to their welfare within the country and stand in place of a family when it comes to care and education and preparation for life and a job. At present no such agencies exist,* although six adoption agencies in the United States work for Korea in the field of adoption. Immigration red tape and Korean red tape make it doubly difficult to bring more than a small number into the United States, however, although there are many American families willing to receive them for adoption. The most successful agency in terms of serving the most children has been and still is the one started by Mr. Harry Holt of Oregon and his family. It is a personal and unorthodox agency, carried on in ways that render the orthodox and conventional agencies frenetic. Many efforts were made in the past to stop Mr. Holt's work and most agencies refused to co-operate with him. Indeed, considerable time and

---

* Since writing the above, I have founded the Pearl S. Buck Foundation, specifically to care for the children of American fathers and Asian women, who must remain in the land of their birth. Its headquarters are in Philadelphia, Pennsylvania.

money were spent to discover the relatively few unsuccessful adoptions Mr. Holt made, in comparison
with the overwhelmingly large number of successful
ones. Even the unsuccessful ones must be measured
against the conditions under which the children would
have been compelled to live, had they not been brought
to the United States. In view of all the voluble criti-
cism, however, I decided to visit Harry Holt and see
for myself.

Thus it came about that not long ago I stood outside
the city of Seoul, Korea, in the bright sunshine of an
autumn morning, and met for the first time someone
whom I had long known. I saw a short stocky man in
late middle age, a plain and honest face made attractive
by a warm smile and lively blue eyes; I felt my hand
seized in a firm and friendly grasp.

"You are Harry Holt," I said.

"Yes."

"We should have met long ago."

"We should have."

It was for me the end of a search. I first heard about
Harry Holt some years ago. The rumors were strange
and unbelievable. An American business man, who
was also a farmer, also a lumberman, was bringing

Korean-American orphans to the United States for adoption. I knew from my own life in Asia that such children are nearly always superior children. Yet I knew, too, that the mixed-race children could not have much hope of a good life unless they were adopted. The ancient countries of Korea and Japan are not accustomed to the half-white in their rigidly organized societies, where even a job depends upon family connections. This means that the half-American children in Asia must grow up as a depressed group. When, therefore, I first heard of Harry Holt and his work for them, I was deeply interested. What was he doing and how was he doing it? Above all, how was he getting it done? He was, frankly, accomplishing much more than all the other agencies put together. Long before I went to see him on that autumn morning I had begun to inquire about him.

The first information I received was, I confess, a shock. It came in the form of a questionnaire, which, it seems, he sent to all prospective parents. To me it was an astonishing document. Very few of the questions related in a material sense to the adoptive family. They pertained to religion and, to my thinking, rather a primitive kind of religion. I had grown up in a missionary environment and had seen and known all kinds of Christians. The questionnaire was distinctly what is called Fundamentalist. Anyone who understands the word as it applies to Christian sects will know what I mean, and to those who do not understand, it does not matter. The point was that Harry Holt was giving children to couples who believed in Christian dogma, and not to others who might be far more worthy of parenthood but who did not so believe. I had seen enough in my lifetime of persons who profess dogmatic religion and do not practice it. I remember that once I protested in an article about Harry Holt, and one day when I was in the offices of the International Social Service, in New York, I asked the executive director if he had heard of Harry Holt and the way he was placing children for adoption. He replied in effect that he had heard, and while he could not approve of placing children in homes merely because those families had certain religious beliefs, yet the sorry fact was that the half-American children in Korea were in such desperate straits that it was better to place them any which way than not at all. Inasmuch as I was not doing anything about the problem at that time, I told myself that I had better say no more about Harry Holt. I determined to find out more about him, and thus began the quiet research which ended on that sunny autumn day in Korea with my coming face to face with Harry Holt.

Meantime the questionnaire continued to trouble me. I could not understand why a man with so good a heart should be so narrow, as I put it, as to say that only families who believed in his kind of dogma could have a child for adoption. I had carried that prejudice for two years or more, when one day a young couple arrived at my door (they had written to ask if they might come and see me). I said they were very welcome, because the young woman was Harry Holt's daughter and the young man was her husband. By this time my research had informed me that Harry Holt was devoting his time and his fortune to the cause of the half-American children in Korea. His two daughters were trained nurses and were helping him. The grateful Koreans adored him and the Korean government had given him their highest decoration in appreciation. I was also informed that American adoption agencies did not approve of him or his methods.

The young couple were now sitting on the couch in front of the fireplace in my library. They wanted to tell me about her father, they said, because he knew that our agency, Welcome House, Inc., was also interested in the American-Korean child. I listened with deep interest, and then asked my unanswered questions.

"Tell me quite frankly why your father sends out that incredible questionnaire to couples who want to adopt a child. Is it possible that he really bases his acceptance of people on whether they believe in dogmatic Christianity?"

The young woman answered. She looked like her father, plain and honest. "It is the quickest way he knows of finding out whether people are good."

"But surely," I urged, "he must know that there are many fine and intelligent people who cannot in honesty answer those questions in the affirmative."

"He knows very well," the young woman said. "He realizes that it is an inadequate method, but he is working alone, he gets no help from other agencies, and in his experience the people who believe in a simple practical Christianity are usually good people and will be good to the child."

"Isn't there a danger that some people who are not good will lie about their beliefs?"

"He knows that," the young man said. "He takes it into account, and he asks for letters about them from other people, too."

I pondered this for a while. I still cannot agree that parents should be chosen for adoptive children through means of a certain religious creed, but, given Harry Holt's circumstances, his passionate conviction that somehow these children must be afforded a chance to live, his belief that we Americans have a responsibility for them, and considering, too, his experience that he could not get any other adoptive agency to undertake this responsibility on a large-enough scale to meet the need even to a fraction, I could but admire his determination to do what he could in his own way.

What he had done was simply beyond praise. He adopted eight of the children himself. He flew to Korea and found out the facts about the others, although he was warned by his doctors that his efforts might end his own life at any moment, for he had a serious heart condition. What he saw in Korea put aside every consideration except that for the children. He found half-American little children in orphanages, many of which were indescribably wretched, but even in the best of them the children were of course deprived of their right to a family life and love. There was very little, if any, overt cruelty, for the Koreans are a kind and gentle people, civilized in heart and mind, but the times were hard, and orphans, Korean or half-American, were too numerous to be accommodated. The half-American children wandered with their camp-follower mothers around the American camps or in villages near where the men were stationed. Not all the mothers are of low class. Korean women are often beautiful and fair-skinned, with brown eyes and soft brown hair. There were couples who fell in love, but could not marry. Illegitimate birth is a catastrophe in Korea, and once it happens, as I have remarked elsewhere, the girl has little or no choice but to become a prostitute. Moreover, South Korea is still so poverty-stricken since the war that everyone has to struggle. In that struggle the half-American child has and will have the least chance.

When Harry Holt realized all this, he simply went to work. He gathered the half-American orphans into a temporary shelter. His daughters helped him, a few American soldiers and others helped him, Koreans helped him; yet mostly alone he tended the children, found medical aid for them, tried to prepare them to pass rigid immigration laws, and brought them as soon as he could to American families. Some, of course, could not meet the test, and he kept those.

He was able to move so quickly and accomplish so much because of the proxy adoption method. By this means a child could be legally adopted by American couples by proxy in Korea and could therefore enter more easily into the United States. It is not a method approved by orthodox agencies, since it means that parents cannot see the child whom they adopt, and if they do not like the child there is no one responsible for its return. The child must stay in the home unwelcome and therefore unhappy. The hard fact was, however, that the proxy method was the only one approved by the Korean government, which at that time was anxious to get the half-American children out of Korea as quickly as possible. Any other method was interminably slow and children often grew too old or died in orphanages before they could get to their American families. In spite of this, American adoption agencies insisted upon the nonproxy method, and many states denied, and still deny, approval to adoption agencies who used the proxy method, thereby compelling half-American orphans to remain in institutions or with their mothers, who may be unable to care for them properly and who may not even want them.

Once more Harry Holt, approved or not, put the children first and faced the practical situation. He enlarged his work, he spent his fortune, he found money from others. While he was doing what we should all have been doing, he continued under heavy attack from the social agencies, who did not approve his methods. Yet whether his methods were good or bad, he was the only person to get the job done. He placed between two and three thousand half-American children in adoptive homes in the United States and he was caring for many more, who perhaps could never be adopted. And all the while he was being accused of malpractice. A research was made by some of the

agencies into unfortunate placements, and a list com-
piled of the alleged homes where families had rejected
a child or ill-treated him. The successful placements
were not mentioned, and the list of unsuccessful ones
was short compared to the many children Harry Holt
had placed. Any approved agency could well have
been proud of the overwhelmingly large proportion of
his successful placements. Moreover, not all of the bad
placements were Harry Holt's and what the report did
not indicate was that he himself would take the child
back if the adoptive parents did not want to keep it.

On that sunny morning in Korea, I put another
question to him. "Why do you let people tell such lies
about you?"

He laughed. "Look at all these children! If I went
around trying to correct the lies that are told about me,
I wouldn't have time for them."

"All these children" was the right phrase. There
were hundreds of them: some of them waiting to be
taken to their adoptive families in the United States;
some of them being fed and healed and encouraged
enough to be adoptable; some tiny newborn babies;
some so crippled and mentally retarded that they could
never be adopted. Just the week before, Harry Holt
had chartered a plane, as he always did, and with the
help of two nurses he himself had taken nearly a hun-

dred children across the Pacific to their waiting families. He had a hard-bitten, wrinkled face, this Harry Holt, but when he tried to tell about those families and the children he would put into their arms, his face broke up.

"There's nothing like a family for a child," he said. "No orphanage compares to it. We try to do what we can here, but our best isn't as good as even a poorish adoptive family. You don't see their little faces light up until they are with a family. I've seen the most miraculous change, even in a month."

The pronoun "we" is right, too. For what I saw in that day I spent with Harry Holt is more than even he could do alone. No one could fail to wonder at and to be grateful for this man and what he accomplished. The first temporary shelter has been superseded by good modern buildings, modest but clean and well kept and excellently managed. A young American doctor and his wife are resident. Nurses in white uniforms and nurses' aides, equally immaculate, care for the children. The aides are young Korean girls, themselves orphans. The diet kitchens, the nurseries, the play rooms and nursery-school rooms, all show loving thought. The children, hundreds of them—too many, too many—are cared for and clean, and run about with a freedom that moves the heart. When Harry Holt appeared they rushed to him, they swarmed over him, they hung on his hands and hugged his legs. He knew each one, it seemed, and he pointed out the ones who would soon be going to their families. That is what he lived for. Of course that great heart of his was open to more than the half-American children.

"You have Korean children here, too!" I exclaimed.

"I never turn away a child," he said simply.

A new building was going up. It was to be a permanent home, he told me, for the mentally retarded, the ones who can never find adoptive homes.

All this is being done at a minimum cost and with much volunteer help, and help from the older children themselves.

"Aren't you happy when you look at all this?" I asked.

He shook his head. "No, not happy enough."

"What more do you want?"

"I want just one thing." He talked with energy, moved with energy, thought with energy.

"What can it be?"

"I want a way of moving these children more quickly to their adoptive homes. I lose too many of them while we are waiting to cut through legal red tape. They die because of red tape. We need a new international adoption law. We have so many tiny babies. See for yourself—most of our rooms have twenty-four babies in them and they should have half that number. Come into my office—"

We went in there and he rummaged among some papers. He handed me four typewritten pages of notes and figures. I cannot of course give in detail what they told me, for space forbids, alas. In summary, however, Page One tells me of four little children, cared for by an eleven-year-old sister in a shack. The youngest is two weeks old. The mother is dead of tuberculosis. The children search garbage piles for food. The baby sucks a rag soaked in rice water as its only food. They were found by American soldiers, who got them into shelter and fed them. But the soldiers could not care for them and appealed to Harry Holt. In six weeks he had an American couple who wanted to adopt all of them. It took ten months to get the adoption papers because an American government official in Japan had to go to Korea to get proof that they were brothers and sisters. The first family were not approved by the United States Immigration and Naturalization Service office. Now a second family have been found but they must be approved by INS. A year and a half has passed and the children are still waiting.

Page Two tells me of the case of little John Kim. He was born on August 7, 1960, and put in an or-

phanage five days later. The mother was Korean,
the father an American soldier. John was a beautiful
baby with blue eyes and red hair. He fell ill with
diarrhea and an infected ear, but was well again in a
month. Meanwhile, within a month Harry Holt found
an American family willing to adopt him by proxy.
But the family had to be approved by INS. During the
next months while John was waiting for his family to
be approved, he contracted a disease prevalent in Korean orphanages, and died.

"It is because of this miserable disease," Harry Holt
said, "that I feel babies must get out of orphanages as
soon as possible and into homes where they can be
protected and receive the love and care they need."

Page Three gives a long list of names, all of babies,
with the number of months of delay between adoption
and the time they were allowed to go to their families.
The months sometimes run into years.

"Tell me what the matter is," I said, "and what we
can do about it."

Harry Holt told me so briefly and concisely that I
knew he had been thinking about it for very long. He
said, in effect:

"The reason for the delay is that the INS performs
a home study on each family and an orphan investigation in the foreign country. The home study is done

only after the adoption is made—very unfortunate, because the orphan waits at least two or three months before he can go to the family. If the petition is refused, then another family has to be found and approved. The rejected family usually gets upset and appeals, which means still more delay.

"Then, too, there's only one man in the whole Far East to do the orphan investigating and that is another reason for delay. He has to see every orphan and of course he has no time to do more, and so he must take the word of the person caring for the child. It's an unnecessary duplication, I think, of the State Department's orphan investigation, and not as thorough . . . I don't see why INS doesn't set reasonable standards and regulations for the international agencies to investigate the family—and *before* the adoption takes place. Older children are psychologically damaged by these delays and disappointments. The agency could be responsible, too, for following up on the child after he comes to the U.S.A.

"Of course agencies don't want to be bothered with more work, and maybe they wouldn't like the rules and regulations," Harry Holt told me. "And there's the problem, still, of the proxy adoption for state welfare agencies. The Children's Bureau in Washington and the Child Welfare League of America and the

International Social Service don't approve of proxy adoptions, and certainly they wouldn't like the agencies who do proxy adoptions. But what can we do? The proxy method helps both child and parents, especially as the foreign countries don't like the nonproxy adoptions, because they fear the child can be too easily switched around later. Here in Korea, for instance, the proxy method is solid. It makes the child truly the son or daughter of the American family.

"Then, too, the nonproxy method is so expensive. The agencies who use it charge just for adoption the same fee that we charge for everything: transportation, visa, passport, medical examination, adoption, home-study fee and care in Korea, all included. And to have one or both parents go to the foreign country to establish residency and then adopt the child is impractical. None but the very wealthy could do it. Then, too —I am sorry to say but it's true—our children could never meet the standards of some of the state agencies, just because they are of a different race from the adoptive parents. I remember that on the back of one of our applications, sent to a state agency, a few words were scrawled: 'We will help to bring a child from Europe, but from Asia? Never!'

"It is our hope and prayer that a really good adoption law will be passed, which will benefit the orphan most of all and also the adoptive parents and the people in the United States. This law should realize the difficulties in caring for children in a foreign country too poor to take care of their own, so that days, weeks, and months of delay may mean disease and sometimes death, and even if the orphan remains physically healthy there could be psychological damage for the child. We would like to see the law give INS responsibility to supervise the international adoption agencies, and the agencies should have the responsibility for the investigation of the family and for the follow-up after adoption. We believe that if INS is instructed to continue investigating the family under the new law, they should do it *before* the adoption takes place. We believe that the State Department's investigation of the orphan is good and that the INS orphan investigation is an unnecessary duplication."

I listened and made my notes. Then I looked at my watch. The day was gone. I had to hurry to other appointments. But I had still a curiosity to satisfy.

"Tell me, Harry Holt, where do you live in the midst of all this?"

He smiled and his eyes suddenly looked very clear and blue.

"Want to see my room?"

"I do indeed."

He led me through endless corridors, the children swinging on his legs and clinging to his hands. He opened a door and there in a neat, sparsely furnished room, bright with late sunshine, I saw some twenty cots. In a corner was one slightly apart, with a table and a few books on it.

"That's my bed," he said. "And these beds belong to some of the little fellows who have fears and slight illnesses. Maybe they need comforting in the night, or maybe a sip of water or a spoonful of cough medicine."

It was the right ending of the day. I came away wondering why on earth we did not all get behind Harry Holt and help him. Proxy or nonproxy, delays and red tape and duplications, why not help that man? He was doing the job, wasn't he?

While I was writing this book, Henry Holt died. Who now will love the children?

The problem of the mixed-race child, born displaced in the world community, must be faced in its entirety. It can be no credit to the United States to have half-American children running about as beggars and potential criminals in the streets of Asian cities and on the islands of the Pacific. To ignore the children, as we are now doing except for the valiant efforts of a few individuals, will solve nothing, either now or in the future. Nor is adoption alone the solution, for as I have said, our severe immigration laws allow only the best and healthiest children to enter our country. This means that the less intelligent, the less attractive, the less able, will be left behind to represent the country of the father.

In India during the centuries when the British ruled, there were of course many half-English children, and until the British left they were a group difficult to assimilate, either by the English or the Indians. These Anglo-Indians, as they are called, wished to be considered English, but this the English would not allow. Now that the English have departed, however, the Anglo-Indians have no choice but to mingle with the Indians, and since the latter have been accustomed to different groups throughout history, the Anglo-Indians are accepted as just another group. This is not the case, at least as yet, in Japan, Korea and other parts of Asia, where the population is homogeneous and all of one color. Indians vary in appearance, from the fair people of Kashmir to the black Jews and the Dravidians of the South. But the child of mixed race in the homogeneous countries faces a hopeless future. I quote from "Children of Tragedy," in a recent report on Intercountry Orphan Adoption, made by the Church World Service Survey Team:

"As human beings we all respond to the challenge of Welcome House: 'When one must choose between social work standards and the life of a child, we choose the life of the child.' And of course a good social worker is flexible enough, and aware enough of the central importance of human life, to adjust procedures to needs and goals and not make methods goals in themselves.

"Would that all of us who must take responsibility for the placement of little children might have some of the experience of Harry Holt! Mr. Holt went to Korea. He lived and slept in the same room with eight and sometimes ten or twelve abandoned babies. He fed them, bathed their emaciated bodies, and did all the intimate, personal things for them that natural fathers often do not do.* He loved the children, and suffered the children, and suffered with them until he could not fail to impress upon those who follow him in his work a desperate urgency to find loving care for babies whose natural parents have forsaken them. For him and for his agency the goal is clear. May the goal be-

* Holt, Mrs. Harry, *The Seed from The East*. (Los Angeles, Oxford Press, 1956).

come clear also to people who have never known the feel of tiny withered bodies, or seen children sitting listless hour after hour, unresponsive, unloved, unable to love.

"If the compelling need to save children could become part of the thinking of the American professional agency, then it might be easier to demonstrate to the Holt Adoption Program, to the Child Placement Service, and to missionaries, the value of methods that really have been developed because they have resulted in the happiest, most successful placement of children. While the visit of the team to Korea was too short, its members saw suffering enough to give them some of that sense of urgency, of the feeling that something must be done both in Korea and in the United States to save thousands and thousands of children from stunted bodies and minds, and also from impersonal, sterile lives in institutions."

VIII

Where Will You Find
Your Child?

What are the adoption agencies, in whose hands lie the fate of thousands upon thousands of children? They are a handful of persons, relatively speaking, but they wield enormous power. They are the ones who decide whether a child shall have the love and care and opportunity that only a good family home can offer, a permanent home, or whether the child is to remain an orphan. They do not move fast enough. "Unfair, unfair," I hear their voices shouting at me. "We can only go as fast as people and laws allow us to move."

Not at all, I must reply. It is the duty of professional persons to lead, not to follow. The choice of following promptly or slowly is the people's but the leadership must be provided by the professionals, and leadership through information and education. If a law is a bad law, if the child's best interests are not of primary importance, the law should be changed, and adoption agencies and their social workers should be the first to move toward change and improvement. Social workers, as I have observed in dealing with them for some thirty years, are almost without exception good persons with real dedication to their work, and even to children. Where I must criticize is in their failure to move with speed sufficient to match the quickly passing years of a child's life. They move slowly because of obsolete laws in the nation and red tape in their own organization. Where, literally, days are important in a child's life they allow weeks and months to pass into years. Where laws are obsolete they should be the first to work for better laws. It is true that they do work for better laws, but too slowly—too slowly. Countless children have remained in orphanages and foster homes because social workers move too slowly. I put these two together, orphanages and foster homes, for while

I grant that foster homes are in some ways better than orphanages if the child is not to have a permanent and real home through adoption, the impermanence of the foster home still makes it little better than the orphanage when one considers that there is permanence in an orphanage. Even the best of foster homes is satisfactory only when it is a place where a child can be cared for in transition. The hope and the goal for the homeless child is always the adoptive family. Without a home, any child is a lost child. In the United States the conservative estimate is that there are three hundred thousand such lost children.

If, upon reading this last sentence, certain couples see the wistful faces, the searching eyes of those hundreds of thousands of children, and feel impelled to adopt one, where should they go to find the child they seek? It is useless to go to an orphanage directly, even though the buildings are crammed with children. No orphanage nowadays has the right to give children for adoption. There is an elaborate ritual, social and legal, to be followed. Parents must brave the ritual to be found in public or private adoption agencies, or they may avoid the ritual and enter the gray market. Let us eliminate the black market, where these babies are sold as merchandise, for it is illegal to sell children in our country. I am glad. It used to be done quite openly in

Asia, especially in times of famine and even to save the life of a child. Thus a starving peasant family might offer a small daughter to a wealthy lady to be her bondmaid: someone less than a daughter but more than a servant. The same thing happens in the United States when a penniless girl finds herself pregnant. She tries to hide her secret but in so doing falls prey to the black marketeer, who takes advantage of her by promising that all expenses will be paid, with an additional sum if she is willing to deliver her child into his keeping. The helpless child is given to the couple who can pay the highest price. Happily the black market scarcely exists today, for new laws make it dangerous for all concerned.

The pregnant girl may, however, go to a doctor or lawyer, asking only that her expenses be paid, in return for which she will give up her child to the paying couple. It is easy for the professional man to agree to this arrangement, for the likelihood is that he has couples among his friends who have asked his help in finding a child for them. This sort of help is called the gray market and it is still rife. Both markets, black and gray, came into existence for two reasons: the lack of a sufficient number of accredited adoption agencies to supply the existing demand for adoptions, and the reluctance of couples to undergo the too often quelling experience they are compelled to undergo in the accredited agency. Adoptive parents are perhaps somewhat oversensitive regarding their childless state and they tend to resent the many questions asked them by social workers, too often young unmarried women, who sometimes seem suspicious of anyone wanting a child.

What of these people who want to adopt children, the men and women who are lonely in their homes unless there is a child, or who, although having children by birth, find their hearts stirred to take some other homeless child for their own? Who are these men and women and why do they want to adopt?

In the first place it is interesting and somewhat dismaying to know that for the first time within memory there are more babies available for adoption than there are parents wanting to adopt. I say babies instead of children, for there have always been more children, not babies, than parents who wanted them. But the babies, the younger the better, have for a long time been in short supply—until now. Among the reasons for the change has been an increase in the birth rate of babies out of wedlock, as well as in the number of children receiving public and voluntary adoption services; a trend for more unmarried mothers to place their children for adoption; modern surgery and psychiatry, which make more children adoptable; new legislation that frees children for adoption if they are permanently neglected by their parents. It seems, too, that there are fewer people in the age group most likely to adopt—the ones from twenty-five to thirty-five years old, who are the so-called Depression children—since doctors have discovered many new ways of solving sterility problems. Moreover, people marry younger than they used to and have children earlier. In larger areas it may be said that the increase in city living, the difficulties of bringing up children in cities, and the economic insecurity of the last ten years have discouraged adoptions. Then, too, the old stigma of childlessness no longer exists. There are men and women now who enjoy living alone together, and make no bones about not wanting children. Added to all this is the uncertainty about a nuclear war and the conviction on the part of fearful people that they do not wish to undertake noncompulsory responsibilities. All in all, the future of adoption is somewhat unclear. It may even be that our communities must prepare other ways of providing home and family environment for the lost child. The sad part of this whole situation is that while there is a plethora of the easy-to-place babies, there is very little hope for the hard-to-place children, the older ones, the handicapped, the ones of mixed race.

Taking all such facts into consideration, there still remain people who want to adopt babies. They are too varied to classify. They belong mostly to the so-called middle class. College people predominate among those who adopt children of mixed race, for prejudice is always stronger in the less educated and less traveled. Most of them are childless, and yet many who have children by birth will add an adopted child to their family. They are almost without exception warm-hearted, outgoing people, happily married, although one occasionally finds a couple on the brink of divorce who are under the illusion that a child will "save" the marriage. Otherwise they all have that indefinable "something" which makes a child happy. I can recognize that "something" at once, and when I do, my impulse is immediately to get them a child. The world is so full of unloved children that not one couple who knows how to love should be wasted. And it is easy to discern when it is not there. Let me illustrate with a small true story. A young couple was once sent to me for acquaintance. It was not my business to approve or disapprove them finally as adoptive parents, for I am not a qualified social worker and I know my own limitations. But I was asked for an opinion. The child in question was a lovely little half-Korean girl, the father an unknown soldier from Virginia. The baby was bewitching, and the couple were obviously enchanted. I was all but melted, when suddenly I saw the young would-be mother look thoughtful.

"Have you a question?" I asked.

She hesitated, then spoke. "Will her eyes change to be more like ours as she grows older?"

"No," I said. "They will only get more beautiful and more Asian."

The conclusion to this story is that they did not get the baby girl. It would not have been fair to her. She deserved a mother who thought her eyes the prettier for being Asian and I am glad to say that soon after she did get such a mother. In such subtle ways hidden prejudices are revealed.

People who want to adopt children are of course of many kinds. Some are timid and self-doubting and these avoid adoptive agencies if possible, as in the case of Mr. and Mrs. Brown, let us say. They are a nice young couple, he an engineer, she a kindergarten teacher. After seven years of waiting for a child and trying every means to have one, they decided to adopt. Would they go to an agency or adopt privately? It is a large question. All adoptive parents seem to dread going to an agency. In some states they have no choice, for, as has been revealed above, there are laws forbidding adoption except through approved agencies. But this young couple lives in California and is allowed a choice. As a famous judge there once put it, "I believe in private adoptions and I believe in agency adoptions. These are matters of temperament and subtlety. They can't always be decided by words or laws. I have found social workers who are skilled, dedicated, hard-working people in the field of adoption, and I have found doctors and lawyers who are equally dedicated, equally hard-working and equally skilled. I believe there is room in this field for both."

Mrs. Brown was pleased therefore when she heard through a friend, himself an adoptive parent and a lawyer, of an unmarried girl who was pregnant and wished to place her child for adoption, and her husband agreed to adopt privately. The lawyer told them about the girl, her looks, her ancestry, her education. He told them, too, about the father. Mr. and Mrs. Brown liked what they heard and decided to take the baby from the hospital if a pediatrician and pediatric neurologist approved. The lawyer then suggested to Mr. and Mrs. Brown that they meet the girl themselves. Mrs. Brown felt that she did not wish to see her, but Mr. Brown went to the lawyer's office and met her, and was reassured.

When Mr. and Mrs. Brown arrived at the hospital after they had been notified of the baby's birth, the natural mother had already gone. The hospital nurse told them to take the baby, the neurologist and pediatrician pronounced her above average, and the happy parents took her home. They say quite frankly that had she not been normal they would not have taken her, and this would have meant that the baby would have been left in the hospital after the mother had gone. The first year was difficult, because the couple knew that at any time for a year the natural mother could change her mind and demand the return of the child. Soon after the child was placed, a social worker was sent by the court to investigate the home. Apparently she was satisfied, since she never returned, and the adoption went through. The couple was much relieved that she did not insist that they move to larger quarters, as they were sleeping in the living room and had given the baby their bedroom. Mr. and Mrs. Brown say that they will adopt again privately, although they are not opposed to agencies. They simply feel that they were more comfortable with this method than with months of interviews and social workers dropping in on them periodically, etc.

Their little girl is two years old and does not look like either parent. She is blond and blue-eyed and both parents have brown hair and eyes. The difference in physical appearance is so pronounced that people constantly ask them, "Where did you ever get that child?" They have become used to this, however, and feel that environmental factors will be more influential in determining the development of the child than any hereditary factors. They admit that they probably took more of a chance adopting privately, that there were more unknowns, but on the other hand they did not care whether or not the child's background approximated their own.

Let us now take the case of Mr. and Mrs. Greene. They tried for several years to have a child, and finally they decided to adopt one. They knew of several couples who had adopted children through a private nonsectarian agency and decided to try this agency. Then a doctor told them of an unwed mother who wanted to place her baby for adoption. They considered this, but finally refused. They felt more secure about adopting through an agency and thought that an agency could be more selective in the choice of a child for them.

Some couples do not enjoy the experience of the agency interviews. One young wife even left the agency offices upon a preliminary exchange with the social worker.

The conversation ran something like this:

"Tell me about yourselves," the social worker began.

"We are just a normal young couple," the wife replied.

The social worker interrupted. "You're not normal or you wouldn't be here."

It was at this point, the young wife said, that she decided to leave.

"For what is more normal for a man and woman in a marriage of love than to want a child?" she inquired of me in recounting the incident.

What, indeed! Happily, Mr. and Mrs. Greene were more fortunate in their next caseworker in another agency. They felt that they learned much about each other through the discussions with her. Mr. Greene felt confident all along that they would get a baby. He felt that they were as good a set of prospective parents as any of the other couples he met at the initial group meeting. Both Mr. and Mrs. Greene felt that they could be perfectly frank with the caseworker. When they were asked what expectations they would have of a child, they felt free to say that they would have higher expectations of a natural child than they would of an adopted child. They felt that they were both intelligent people with high demands on each other, therefore they would have had similar expectations of a natural child. But they felt that they could not have such expectations of an adopted child, since they would know little of the child's heritage. They said they would be pleased if the child were very intelligent, but not disappointed if it were average. When they were asked if they preferred a child of their own religion, Mrs. Greene said she did not care. Mr. Greene, however, preferred that the child be Protestant.

Six months after they applied they were called and told that the agency had a little girl for them. She arrived when she was three and a half months old. She had been a premature baby and had been kept at the hospital for several weeks and then placed in a foster home for nine weeks, where she was under careful medical observation. The foster mother wrote a careful letter to the adoptive parents about the baby's development and personality. The parents found this very reassuring, as they were uneasy about adopting a three-and-a-half-month-old baby rather than a newborn, and wondered what experiences the child had had in the foster home.

Mr. and Mrs. Greene did not want to know anything about the baby's parentage. They were even disturbed that because Mrs. Greene was musical, the agency told them that the child's parents had been musical. They wanted no information which would "concretize" the image of the natural parents. After the child arrived they were unprepared, too, for some of the reactions of other people. The most unwelcome comment was the persistent question, How could a mother ever give up a darling little baby like that?

They will apply for another child when the little girl is two, since a two-year waiting period between applications is a regulation of their agency. This agency has recently increased from two to three the number of children which it will place with a couple and Mr. and Mrs. Greene will try to adopt three children.

IX

White, Gray or Black Market

Each adoptive couple is different from every other in personality and desires, but they have in common the longing for a child, and they have to make the decision whether to use an agency or adopt privately through a friend, doctor or lawyer. Pediatricians, if consulted, usually say that a good agency placement is preferable to private placement. It affords the natural mother the opportunity to work through her problems, cope with her guilt, and make her plans for the baby with a trained social worker. If the child should be born with a handicap, the agency will care for the child and help to place it. With private placement there is no recourse. If no adoptive parents will accept a handicapped child, that child is returned to the natural mother, who is not prepared for the burden, has no place to turn, no money to support the child. If the girl is uncertain as to whether or not she wishes to give up her baby, the agency will arrange for the child to be placed in a foster home until she decides, so that with the agency placements there are fewer cases of the mother requesting the return of the baby. From the point of view of the adoptive parents, the agency has a selection of children to choose from when it makes a placement, whereas the doctor or lawyer knows of only one baby and one set of adoptive parents. The agency can investigate the background of the child, can estimate the intelligence of the mother and ascertain her temperament. It is important to know something about the child's heritage before selecting the right home.

Let parents take their choice between agency or private adoptions. I agree with the judge in California. Each has its advantages and disadvantages. It may be said, however, that agencies are being forced to be less rigid than they once were, less restrained by red tape, more conciliatory and even welcoming toward couples seeking a child, now that they are beginning to need such couples and there is no longer a shortage of babies.

Indeed, their whole approach to the job will have to be revised, not to say reformed, and the reform must begin within themselves, in their own attitudes. Social workers vary, as do all other persons. Some are both wise and kind, and some are not. Whatever they are, they will have to learn how to investigate with tact, question with respect, and decide without demanding perfection. The basis upon which decision must be made is whether the child would be better off where it is—in orphanage or temporary foster home—and the answer is usually in the negative. As I have said elsewhere and here repeat, a foster home is never secure and the child knows it. At any moment the foster family may give him up. This may even be used as a threat. Unorthodox though it may be, I question sometimes whether an orphanage is not better for the child than the foster home, for at least the orphanage has a sort of permanency, however impersonal. A foster home demands even more of a couple than an adoptive home. It is rare to find women who are so overflowing with natural love that they can love a child unreservedly, though temporarily, because they love all children—past, present and future. But most women hold back their emotions, in self-protection. "I can't let myself get attached, because I won't always have this child" is their attitude. They can scarcely be blamed, and yet the child feels the detachment. He dreams of a mother and father who is his "for keeps." There is no substitute for permanent, loving parents.

No, the foster family is not the answer for the problem of the homeless child. What *is* the answer? It must still be found, I believe, by the trained professional, aided, abetted and prodded by the concerned lay citizen in the community. A few years ago, thus concerned, I wrote the following, which is an excerpt from an article on the subject:

Why, one wonders, have social agencies not reformed their own procedures? An increasing number of angry and resentful people, who even when approved must wait long for a child while in the meantime they see orphanages and institutions flourishing, will certainly find an outlet by taking matters into their own hands. I can attribute unrealistic attitudes of agencies to two factors: first, mediocre quality of the average social worker as a person—and to this there are many exceptions—and second, to the inadequate education which they receive in schools of social work.

How does one discern the mediocre person? The best test is to ask whether he is informed by techniques or confined by them. A mediocre person learns by rule and by rote and he practices by rule and by rote. Such persons function well in routine jobs, yet nothing to do with adoption can be routine, since here human beings are concerned at their tenderest points, babyhood and parenthood. Social workers ought therefore to be of the highest caliber or they do great damage through injustice and prejudice.

The profession of social work is a noble one, demanding high integrity, broad understanding and a tender heart. I should like to see adoption workers chosen primarily from among older people. Women whose children are grown and who still find themselves young enough to learn are ideal material for adoption workers.

The curricula of our schools of social work, alas, need severe revision. More and better courses in psychology and indeed in all subjects leading to the understanding of human beings and far less emphasis on technical procedure are what I should like to see. The consultants for such revision should not be other social workers exclusively and certainly none but the older and experienced social workers. I should like to see a widely chosen group of citizens, all parents, meet with a group of educators, lawyers and elder social workers to plan new curricula in adoptive theory and practice for schools of social work.

Above all—oh, very much above all—I should like to see the spirit of service to humanity restored somehow, whatever the subject. The young social worker today, man or woman, too often comes out of his school of social work as coldly professional as a union worker. He does not think of the job as an opportunity for service and certainly not—at least visibly— of the need. He thinks of his benefits, his prestige, his salary, his hours, his vacations, his retirement plan. These are important and should be thought of but he should take a minimum for granted and put his mind and heart on what he can do for human beings—to be old-fashioned about it.

Unless professional people keep in mind that they are servants of humanity, they are not good professionals and certainly they cannot solve the monstrous problems of humanity. Idealism? Certainly, for we cannot live without it. Idealism is the prerogative of the human being. It is the chief difference between man and beast. It is indispensable in the handling of children.

How can the social worker assume the leadership so much needed in his field? Well, he can act individually with idealism and he can influence his agency so to act. He can reach to every other agency with his idealism and especially to such central organizations as the National Child Welfare League, requiring of them more than mere co-ordination and approval. He should ask for leadership from those who should lead.

Demand creates supply. At present there is no leadership, worthy of the name, in the field of child adoption.

What would leadership, worthy of the name, work for first of all?

The goal is a free child, freed for parents, love and home. The way to achieve the goal is first through new unified laws—laws which, crossing state and county limits, will make it possible for adoption agencies to search the nation for the right child for the right home. There ought to be a national pool of children and another of adoptive parents and information about them flowing freely through all professional centers of adoption. There is talk of such a pool, but it has not progressed much further.

Second, both law and adoption professions should work to defend the child against the divisions of religious groups. Fortunately there are within these groups many sincere and enlightened members who would help and who need only to be informed.

Third, the boards of trustees and directors of adoption agencies should assume responsibility for the outlook and performance of professional agencies under their care. Too often the citizens on these boards are themselves provincial in mind and concerned chiefly with petty finances and procedures. They need to be replaced by citizens who are able to fulfill the real responsibilities, of their office. The duty of a board is more than hasty and superficial meeting over minutes and budgets; its duty is constantly to measure the achievement of the agency against the goal, which is the placing of every orphaned child in a good and loving family.

No limitations of religion, race or geography should exist to prevent the reaching of the goal. And citizens must keep the goal always clear for the professionals, and good professionals must create the best techniques for the citizens.

Let no small arguments be raised here. It is idle to retort, for example, that adoptive parents usually want a perfect child, that most children are not perfect, and so on. Parents want a child for a child's sake. They can be helped to want a handicapped child, a child of mixed origin, any child at all. Parents need guidance in finding out the depth of their own love for a child. All good social workers know it and some of them practice this kind of humanity.

I feel no need to revise these remarks. They still hold true. I amend them only to say again that social workers are themselves beginning to recognize the need for change in themselves and in their training, in order to meet the change in our society. The increase in numbers of homeless, unwanted children—a result of the sexual freedom between modern men and women—is attended by a decrease in the number of adopting parents. The predicament must be faced squarely by the professionals. New solutions must be found. If our American way of life fails the child, it fails us all. Leadership must be provided by the professional, especially since in spite of all difficulties it appears that most couples wishing to adopt a child start their search with private or public agencies, where such agencies are available. There has been a great deal of publicity about the insecurity of private placements and the protection that agencies can afford because they take custody of the child before placing it for adoption. As between the private and public agency, it seems the private is preferred, probably because of some status symbol or appeal to many people in going to the private agencies, since traditionally in adoption circles it is recognized that private agencies can, and must, select the children it will take under their care. The private agency usually takes care of the "blue ribbon" children. This is not always true of course, but by and large, it is a necessity for a private agency to be extremely careful about the children coming under its care. Such an agency does not have the wide base of public-tax financial support. The agency must examine the possibility that children with many unknowns in their backgrounds can be "unadoptable" and become the lifelong responsibility of the agency. This is costly and can greatly limit an agency's service to adoptable children.

In general, the agency placement appeals to the couple who wants legal protection and who understands what this protection can mean; to the couple who would like to have a great deal of information about the background of the child, and assurances about the child's background and paternity; and to the couple who wants to feel assured that the natural mother of the child has received counseling services and has made a thoughtful and final decision about releasing her child. Many couples feel they wish the comfort of knowing that the mother has been given every service possible and has made a decision after having considered every possible alternative.

There are couples who like to have the security of having a child who has been psychologically tested and professionally observed and examined so that there is some assurance that the child is normal, physically and mentally, and if not normal, that the child can be returned to the care of the agency before the final adoption and without court action involving the natural mother.

Some couples wish, too, the security of a continuing

service to the adoptive family in the form of casework supervision of the placement, and the sharing of the joys and problems which arise. There is added security in an agency placement if there are extensive medical and special expenses incurred for the care and treatment of the child previous to the finalization.

Who are the families attracted to independent, gray-market placements? They may be families who have been rejected by an adoption agency for some reason, or who have been unable to secure the services of an agency, or are impatient with the policies and practices of agencies, or have never sought out an agency, but are offered a child for adoption from a private source before they reach an agency.

Besides these, there are others turning to independent adoptions who have already sought out private agencies or public agencies to study them in an effort to secure a child, but have been unable to get an agency to study their home and have therefore been compelled to turn to independent adoption. These are usually couples of mixed marriage, the difference being either a difference of race or religion, or only of a religion which the agency does not consider. Or they may be couples who have reached an age beyond that acceptable to an agency, or they may already have a family of children. Service families who have to move about, or adoptive fathers who are in hazardous occupations are often unacceptable to agencies.

The result is that many couples who would prefer to adopt through an agency, desiring the protection that an agency could offer them, when given the choice between having no child at all and having a child adopted without these protections, will resort to independent adoption. It must be stated realistically, too, that there are places in the United States where there are no authorized adoption agencies. It must also be realized that there are sections of this country where there are authorized adoption agencies, but where these agencies cannot serve all couples because of lack of financial means.

There are also couples who have had an unpleasant experience with an agency and have turned from this experience to seek a child through independent adoption placement. There have even been couples who have been misinformed, or hearing stories from other couples, they have formed a prejudice without an experience with an adoption agency, and have decided they will not turn to the agency for help. Some couples therefore feel they do not want or need agency protections and they are willing to take their risks until the time the child is finally adopted, or to adopt the child knowing there may be weaknesses in the legal finalization due to the manner in which the child was released, or the manner of placement.

There are, too, a number of adoptive couples who have never actually gone to an adoption agency either public or private, because they have been offered children by friends or relatives, or by interested doctors. There are also a number of doctors who, when they realize their patients are having difficulty having children or when they know it might be impossible for their patients to have children, will volunteer to seek a child for the couple, or will offer them a child who needs a home. It is extremely difficult for a couple who wants a child to consider the pros and cons of the various types of adoption when a child is actually being offered to them, and many do accept. These children could be studied and approved by adoption agencies, both public and private, if agencies were on the alert, but agencies are so few, relatively speaking, that there are many places in the United States where this private placement is the only kind of adoption possible because there are not agencies available to offer services. Adoption service is the most expensive type of social service, with the exception of psychiatric services. There are places where adoption agency service cannot be offered because of lack of community support and funds.

All in all, it must be remembered that were it not for

independent placements, many children now happy in adoptive families would be orphans. Before condemning such independent placements for adoption one must consider the alternative. Since there are not enough agencies to render adoption services either to available children or to couples seeking children to adopt—nor are they likely to be numerous in the foreseeable future, under the present population growth—the reasonable course would be to recognize the inevitable existence of the gray market and supply legal fortification for it, with protection for child and parents. This is all the more necessary because it is quite true that there are certain children whom the average adoption agencies will not accept, and the unmarried mother is compelled to resort to the gray market. There are children who are not accepted by private agencies for a number of reasons, and these children are not acceptable to the public agencies for various other reasons. For example, when a pregnant girl comes to a maternity home, or some other type of shelter, extremely late in her pregnancy, there are agencies which on principle will not accept this child's care. The agency feels they need the protection of a period of time for working with the mother, time to gather history, both medical and social. One may ask, What becomes of this child? The desperate mother resorts to an independent placement, if possible. A child of mixed racial extraction is a problem, too, for the name agency, especially if there is some Negro extraction or other equally hard-to-place extraction, such as Portuguese or Mediterranean Italian or Oriental or Indian. Or the child may have some health problem in his background which may make him hard to place. These health problems can include all of the diseases which are believed to be hereditary and those which are suspected to be hereditary, such as epilepsy or some diagnosed schizophrenia or other mental disorder that is believed to be hereditary, and a variety of other health problems.

Sometimes agencies refuse a child whose paternity is in question. There are instances where the mother of a child will confide to the agency that she is uncertain about the paternity of her child, or that one of several men may possibly be the father, and then the agency may feel it cannot accept custody. If there is any suspected incest in a child's background, most private agencies will not accept custody of a child for fear that the child cannot be placed. There are, too, a number of natural mothers who will not consider releasing their child to an agency. Many of these girls are reluctant to consider an agency, believing the child may be placed in an institution or face long-term foster care. Such girls usually wish to seek an independent placement for their child, where they can be assured the child will go to the adoptive home from the hospital. Also involved in the decision of some girls to seek such placement is the fact that some girls refuse to relinquish their child to a private agency when actual appearance in court is required. Some cannot emotionally face the finalization of this step and for a variety of reasons refuse to consider any agency where a court appearance is necessary. Included here is the underage girl—eighteen in some states, twenty-one in others—who will not let her family know of her pregnancy, thus cannot have them appear in court with her to relinquish her rights. She may turn to an independent placement to avoid this. So also may a married woman whose legal husband is not the child's actual father. She may not wish her legal husband to co-sign the required release of a private agency. When a child is released to an agency the written consent of all parties who have any right to or responsibility for the child must be secured.

In summation, it is safe to say that in many places in the United States the only agency is the public one. When there are both public and private adoption agencies, public agencies would probably serve those couples who cannot afford the fees charged by private agencies. Generally speaking, there is fair co-operation between the agencies, but the fact remains that however adequate the agencies are in a community and however well they perform, private placements still take place, except in the states where they are illegal. It appears then, that the gray market satisfies the needs of some persons.

Among professionals concerned with adoption we must also consider the judges. Of judges I have known many. They are all individualists, and seldom pay much attention to the law. They have the right to set it aside, it seems, and they often do set it aside. They are dreaded and loved, very much as doctors are. Those dependent upon their decisions gauge their moods, and carefully refrain, if possible, from bringing up cases on bad days. Social workers soon learn their foibles and cater to them instinctively. Such social workers have my sympathy. To work for months on finding a child and parents who seem properly to belong together, only to have a judge unaccountably set the whole matter aside because of some prejudice of his own results in multiple disaster. I will illustrate from two incidents in my own experience.

There was once a fine young Jewish couple who wished to adopt a mixed-race baby girl. The baby's mother was Protestant-American, the father was Buddhist-Japanese. Neither cared what the religion of the adoptive parents was, so long as they were kind and good. This they were, and more besides, but they lived in New York City, where there is congregated the greatest number of judges in the world—and of the greatest variety, temperamentally and otherwise. As the day of adoption drew near I became increasingly nervous. Would the judge decide against an adoption so religiously and racially mixed? I learned the name of the judge and discovered to my fright that he was Irish and Catholic. I like Irish and Catholic, I hasten to say, but it added another ingredient to our already mixed situation. I decided that I myself had better be present at the adoption and do what I could, if anything, in case the judge looked ominous at some point.

We arrived—social worker, parents, baby girl by now a year old, and myself. The baby was a picture in a white organdy frock with ribbons. She was active and gay and ran about while we waited. And we did wait, for two and a half hours, until the judge was ready for our case. By this time the small girl was no longer fresh or in a gay mood. Her ruffles were gray with city soot and she was bored with the whole situation.

When we arrived before the judge we could not be sure of his mood, either. He examined the parents before him and stared over his glasses at the young parents and the squirming baby in their arms. A few questions might have sufficed, but when he put a question as to their religion, the agitated couple hastened to explain that they were not orthodox and were perfectly willing to bring up their little girl in any religion required.

This was exactly the wrong position, as instantly became evident. The judge took off his spectacles and launched into a sermon, the gist of which was that they must bring up the child in a religion, whatever it was, for without religion they were not worthy as parents. He became impassioned and eloquent and went on at great length. It was the little girl who then took matters into her own hands by beginning to bellow so loudly that we could not hear the judge, whereupon he drew to a quick conclusion and approved the adoption. The moral of this incident for me was that judges are sometimes, maybe often, much better than one fears.

The second judge was a difficult one. He had a reputation, and again we had a mixed-race child to place with a white family. Would he or would he not, etc.? This time, being more seasoned and fatalistic, I decided not to be present. The social worker reported to me later that for a time it seemed the judge would not allow the adoption. Only after long and tedious questioning and much soliloquizing did he do so. I felt impelled to visit him after it was all over, for his interpretation of our Pennsylvania adoption law was so unique that I wanted an explanation.

Once in his office I was frank and he responded with equal frankness. I summoned courage.

"But, Judge," I remonstrated, "we have many adoptions and see more than a few judges, and you are the only one who interprets the law in this way."

"I don't know how the rest of them interpret it and I don't care," he retorted, his Pennsylvania-Dutch chin very firm.

"Do judges never get together when a law is passed?" I inquired.

"What for?" he asked.

"To decide together what it means," I suggested.

"No," he said shortly.

"Then you should," I went on, with temerity, I confess, for who am I to argue with a judge? "You should get together whenever a new law is passed and agree on its interpretation, at least minimally, so that the rest of us know what to expect. A law is a law, or it isn't. We ought to be able to know."

I still think it is a good idea for judges to agree together on the usages of a law. As it is now, judges have too much individual power.

Let us review the situation. We are in the initial stages of a sexual revolution. There are approximately 250,000 children born out of wedlock each year in the United States. In 1938 the number was approximately 88,000. Last year about 107,000 children were adopted. The remaining ones are in foster homes, hospitals and orphanages. Of the 107,000 adopted last year, 49,000 were adopted by relatives, and of the remaining 58,000, 60% were adopted through agencies and 40% by independent placements. That is, the mother preferred not to go to an agency but to allow a doctor or lawyer or friend to place her baby. This is called the gray market.

The black market is almost out of existence, thanks to the strong attack upon it by agencies some years ago. Of course as a result of such agency efforts and of co-operating private efforts, all independent adoptions have been seriously curtailed. This has been accomplished mainly by the passing of a law permitting only agency placements, and the effect of such a law is illustrated by the case of Connecticut, where in 1959 there were 1,092 adoptions, of which 58% were independent or private placements. After the passing of the law prohibiting all but agency placements, in 1960 agencies placed 96% of all adoptions, but only 573 adoptions were made, and of these almost half were made the year before. Similar circumstances occurred in Delaware, where the number of adoptions fell from 254 in 1959 to 144 in 1960, and 128 in 1962.* Other states seem inclined to follow the example of these two, encouraged by the United States Children's Bureau, which hopes that its proposed legislative package will become law in all states, thereby permitting only agency adoptions, and demanding that when parents' rights are relinquished, children be given by the court to agencies only.

In short, every effort is being made to insist that the agency be the sole instrument for the adoption of children. Such requirements as the natural mother returning after a year to declare her willingness for the adoption, or an early registration of the child in an adoptive home, make independent placements difficult indeed. Often the mother is afraid to appear in court and thus reveal her identity, or she cannot be found. Moreover, agencies are reluctant to recognize any attempt to legalize independent placements, since they are convinced that they themselves should be the sole agents in the adoption field. One would be inclined to agree with them, for certainly adoptive parents should feel more

* See article by Rose Jean Isaac in *The Atlantic Monthly*, November, 1963.

secure in knowing that they are protected by experts. The hitch is that while the agency placements are undoubtedly safer than individual ones, the harrowing truth is that agencies cannot do the job. One has to take the choice of knowing that about half of the available children are well placed and the other half not placed at all, or half are well placed and the other half perhaps not all so well placed, but still better off than they would be in hospitals, orphanages and foster homes. Before laws are passed restricting adoptions to agencies, it would be only realistic to determine if there are enough agencies to place all available children. As it is, the future looks dark indeed, because of the dwindling supply of adoptive parents.

Nor can we suppose that agency placement is always wise. Social workers frequently disagree on the applicant parents. A couple may be accepted by one social worker and rejected by another for the flimsiest and most whimsical of reasons or even because of prejudice, conscious or unconscious. One agency may reject a couple *in toto* and another may accept the same couple, although an agency rejection is like a prison sentence—it stalks the couple and sometimes discourages them completely, so that a good home for a child is lost. Social workers and judges in our society are given an omnipotence assumed elsewhere only by bloody dictators. The only hope at present is that the increasing oversupply of children will force a new realism upon these arbiters so that freer and less rigid demands will be made on persons wishing to adopt children.

One of the most preposterous of these demands, next to that of religion, is the demand for absolute proof of infertility. In the first place there can be no such proof, short of removing the reproductive organs. Often the adoption itself and the relaxation of having a child in the house will at last cause a pregnancy. Yet the demand is made, and sometimes with such insistence that the adoptive parents withdraw rather than submit to indignities and violation of privacy. A study made in Pittsburgh of Negro couples interested in adoption— a much-needed group, since most Negro orphans never find adoptive homes—revealed that the greatest single reason for such withdrawal was the agency's demand for proof of infertility. Of the whole group studied, only 20% of those who applied finally received children. Yet, with less rigidity and, it may be added, more common sense, the ratio might have been increased. Part of the lack of realism in social workers is due to their youth and to their zeal to follow school instructions to the letter. Yet no experience is more heartbreaking for an adult couple, warm-hearted and mature, than to realize that their fate depends upon a young woman with little or no experience of life. They may recognize her sincerity and even respect it, but it is agony, nevertheless, to know that their home may be forever empty, their marriage never blessed by a child, because of this same earnest young thing—or old one.

X

The Nature of Love

There is as yet no means of prevention perfect enough short of sterilization, to guarantee that no child will result from the physical union of a man and a woman. Technical means are ignored in moments of emotion and unexpected impulse, or even of laziness and carelessness. Certainly in this era of changing attitudes and shifting standards, no amount of frank warning and availability of birth control implements have served to prevent the birth of two hundred and fifty thousand children who have no families. Our society apparently is not ready for this child. He is called illegitimate when he is born and the weight of his illegitimacy is his life-long burden. Even if he is adopted, his birth will be flung at him by cruel people. I shall never forget the day when my eight-year-old son came in from school, his eyes blazing, his blond hair a tangle. He flung his books on the floor.

"Who is my real mother?" he shouted.

"I am," I said. "I am your real mother, by love and by law."

He glowered at me. "At school they say you're not! They say my mother was the town whore. What's a whore?"

I put everything aside. We went into a long conference and I established, I hope, a basis of understanding for the future. For it was not the only time that such cruelty had occurred.

And then when the day drew near for my daughter's marriage, there was the question of her heredity. She brought it up, she said, because she felt the father of her children-to-be had the right to know what stock she came from. It was of the best, I was able to tell her, but I knew that by herself she would never have thought of it. Someone else, some relative of the bride-groom, had put the cruel query. I took the precaution myself of telling my future son-in-law what fine ancestry his children would have. He said immediately what I knew he would say, but which I wanted to hear said: that nothing mattered except that he loved her. But it was all cruel, and all part of the burden that we place upon some quarter of a million of our children every year, and this in spite of the fact that many of them are adopted into good and loving homes. The adoptive parents forget that the child is not born of their flesh. They take the child as their own and he becomes their own. Yet, though the child may and usually does respond with all his heart, accepting them wholly, our society still forces them to remember and to inquire of themselves who they are.

Such periods of inquiry usually come three times, the first when school life begins, the second in adolescence and the third at the time of marriage. Each time must be met with love and patience—and suffering. For the adoptive parents suffer, too, not only for the child's sake, but also for their own. There is a rending of the flesh and a breaking of the spirit when the child asks the cold questions, "Who am I? Why am I here?"

Somehow or other we must change this situation. When a child is born he is already a human being, and as such he has a right to the opportunities and joys of life. He should not be burdened with the cruel circumstances of his birth, over which he has no control. There is no such person as an illegitimate child and this has often been truly said. He appears according to the laws of nature. What is illegitimate is the condemning environment into which he is born. Innocent though he is, he is born guilty of a crime he has not committed. He suffers for it all his life. Even though he learns through maturity to accept what he is and to accommodate himself to the facts, yet in his secret heart is the eternal *why* of his birth. Why did those two persons, his natural father and mother, create his being? Why, having done so, did they reject him? Above all, why did his mother give him away? However much one explains the agony of the giving, however one mouths the usual phrases—"she had no home for you," "she thought it would be better for you to have a real home and parents who could love you and take care of you"—the secret heart believes that she could have thought of some way if she had wanted to do so. Yet the fact is that in our present society there is no way for the unwed mother to keep her child. For if she keeps him the burden still falls on the child. "Who is your father?" The question in itself is a cruel accusation. The unhappy mother may concoct a fantasy of the father's death, but she cannot maintain it. Sooner or later the wise child discovers the fraud. Then the old demand returns: "Why did they let me be born?"

The answer, if the unwed mother is honest, is that

she could not help it. She tries in every way she knows to prevent the birth, but she does not succeed.

If possible, there is a marriage. But sometimes she is mature enough, however few her years, to know that there should not be a marriage. She realizes that she has entered into a physical relationship that can never grow into other areas—of mind and spirit. Such a marriage is no foundation for a home and she refuses it. Sometimes she accepts it at any cost and with a permanent unhappiness, which cannot provide the child with the atmosphere he needs for full development, but which at least spares him the accusation of being illegitimate. Sometimes she tries to stop the child's being born. She tries abortion.

Abortion has been called "one of the great epidemic diseases of our time." Of all the natural deaths in New York City in 1962, more than half were from criminal abortion. It is said that there are more than 1,200,000 abortions, or attempted abortions, in the United States every year. That is, for every fourth birth there is an abortion. One hospital in New York City reports six or seven abortions a day. We may expect a rising number, for in the days of pre-Castro Cuba, women went there to have the operation performed. Since abortion is illegal in the United States except for medical reasons, women now resort to criminal abortion, at the risk of their lives. The woman who seeks such an abortion is not always unwed. She may be married and not wish to have the child, or the child's father—increasingly likely in these days of sexual revolution—may not be her husband. Her child will then be as illegitimate as though she were unwed.

What is the answer? Various nations have tried to find it. Asia segregated male and female at an early age and maintained a strict guard over the female. But modern ways are influencing even ancient Asia and it is only a question of time and rising industrial life before they will face the same problems that we in the West have. Young women in India and Japan are flocking into offices and factories, where they work side by side with young men. Japan is trying legalized abortions and is managing at least to keep her population stable. However, since there are not enough legalized abortions even then to cope with unwanted pregnancies, illegal operations continue in ever-increasing numbers. Sweden tries to solve the problem by recognizing the unwed mother and her child as respectable citizens, but if this is done on a wide scale we shall see a return to matriarchy, to the home and the family where the man is not essential except as a stud animal. This I consider a real threat to our society. I believe that the most successful civilizations, in human terms, are those which have come the closest to achieving real understanding and mutual appreciation between men and women. The American family at its best is a unit unsurpassed in my observation. The problem is, today, how to maintain it at its best, when the new sexual freedom allows women to be promiscuous. For whether a woman has one affair or twenty, it is the same promiscuousness. She has shown herself available.

"It is a strain for a man to live in New York," an attractive middle-aged man confessed to me once. "There are so many available women here."

"Married or single?" I inquired.

"It makes no difference," he said. "They are equally available."

We talked for a while of what it means to a society when its women make themselves "available." We agreed that it was a sign of the breakdown of the family as we know it. For our family system is expressed in patriarchal terms. Man's nature is such that he remains within the family system only when he is head of the family and responsible for its support and existence, and is essential to the family. If he absents himself, if he is irresponsible, if he is promiscuous, the family, and with it society, drifts into a matriarchy because the woman is thereby compelled to assume full responsibility. Industrialization tends to bring about this drift, for with the present high cost of living, an increasing number of women are leaving the home to work outside. This in itself removes part of the responsibility for the family from men, and if the woman earns more than the man, may entirely absolve him from responsibility. So profound, so complex, and yet so tenuous is the relationship between man and woman that the two will certainly draw apart unless they are united by more than physical bonds, or even by their parental duties.

A man's relation with his own child, if his position is minimized, dissolves rather easily. I have observed this in divorced couples. There is often a passionate determination on the part of the father at first to keep his hold on the children. The law is against him, of course, for it recognizes the mother's claim as supreme, unless she is proved unfit. At any rate, it is not long before the father, in his new freedom, begins to see his children less and less often, until at last they all but cease to see him and he remembers but forgets. I sometimes wonder if, after all, the family is not an artificial unit, a relic of the days when man was the hunter of food, the hewer of wood and the drawer of water for the woman and child. Yet I know it is not so. I know that the only completely happy life for man and woman is their life first together and then with their children. I firmly believe that no marriage can be really happy, and no home a happy one for the children as well, unless woman puts man first and man puts woman first, each for the other the giver of every good gift. Children are the fruit of this total love, but children are not to take first place in the woman's heart. That belongs to the man. When woman allows the helplessness of a child to creep into that center sacred to man, it is an usurpation, and the home and the family are undermined.

All this is preliminary for solution. We shall not see a change in our society until we see a change in our education. Women should be educated for men, and men should be educated for women, for in the other and with the other, each finds his and her own fullest development. At present we have no such education. Yes, I know that we have sex education in many of our schools, but sex education as it is now taught is not what I mean. I said education of men and women for each other, and physical sex is only a part of the whole, and perhaps a lesser part. I will not forget the day when a certain young daughter of mine came home from school, threw her books on the table and burst into tears. Upon my solicitous inquiry she replied:

"I do wish they wouldn't keep trying to teach sex at school," she sobbed. "It takes all the romance out of love."

What they should have been teaching was love between the sexes. And what is that love? It is more than the mating instinct, it is more than physical sex, but it includes both. It is the most complete relationship in human life, and merely to teach the physical and technical does indeed rob love of its heart and soul. True education for life begins, I believe, in the recognition that men and women are totally different from each other. They look at the same scenes and see them differently. When both are artists dealing with the same human stuff as their material, they create differently. In this is the value of sex. What men and women become as a result of their difference, what they create out of the combination of their differences in complementation, creates wholeness. Without combination and complementing, creation is warped and one-sided, whether that creation be music, painting, writing, politics and national life—or a child.

For when I say creation, I mean the word in a global sense, beginning in the home and encompassing every phase of life in the universe. A woman can and should, if she has the confidence of man, move into every area of human existence and yet remain a woman. Indeed, she loses her value if she becomes less. We hear the complaint these days that women are becoming masculine and men are becoming effeminate, that is to say, unmasculine, weak, etc. I am amused when I hear this complaint. Is woman indeed so powerful in her nature that she compels men to become weak? If so, is not man then inherently weak? Such questions are idle, for the complaint is idle. If woman must be kept segregated and subdued, a sex symbol instead of a whole woman, in order that man may maintain his strength and his position, then he is indeed the inferior. But I do not believe that either sex is inferior to the other. Each has its individuality and each is necessary to the other in every aspect of life. We need to know what the individuality is, however, in order to instruct our young in the functions of sex in its totality. And they must be taught to realize that the totality is never achieved, with its maximum of sexual enjoyment, unless knowledge is complete.

I do not believe in segregation of the sexes, as practiced in Asia. On the contrary, I believe in nonsegregation at all levels, from birth to death. Men and women should face life together, solve its problems in the firm belief that solutions can be found in their combined knowledge, judgment and energy, and enjoy the rewards the more because they work together for solution and enjoyment. Man and woman can do this only when they freely allow each to be himself, herself, without strictures and division of duties. There are some women who are better ditch-diggers than some men. Therefore, let them be ditch-diggers! Some men are better housekeepers than women. Therefore, let them be housekeepers! But allow the woman to dig the ditch in her own way, and the man to keep house in his own way. This they must, out of the difference in their natures.

What needs to be done now is to explore those two differing but complementary natures, those two attitudes toward life which, combined, make the total view. Alas, we have no such literature to help us in our society. Of books on sex there is a plethora but they deal primarily with physical sex, whereas the truth is that we cannot understand or even experience physical sex fully until it takes its place in the whole relationship that knits man and woman into one being. Woman must be wooed, these books suggest, in order that she respond satisfactorily to man in the act of physical sex. Yet if this be the only purpose of the wooing, she will still not respond, except superficially. She will respond to man's full content only when the physical act comes as the expression of a complete life with him in all areas.

Nor is it always the man who must woo. Woman is quite capable of using her body to attract him, and indeed she is so taught to do in the shallows of our modern civilization. He may yield, but it will not be to her content, for man, too, does not live by flesh alone. He discards woman after he discovers that there is no more to her than "a rag and a bone and a hank of hair."

This I believe is what we must teach our young male and female. With full knowledge of each other, with respect for the individual, and with the desire for each to develop to full capacity, neither shaping nor being shaped, man and woman learn to live in co-operation. For the nature of man and woman is manifold in function. I stood in recent months at the entrance to the Elephanta Caves near Bombay, India. Long ago the caves were made into a vast temple. There, facing me as I entered, was a monumental image of the deity. It is a great head with three faces, so huge that it towered above me into the lofty ceiling. I examined these faces. The central one was the strongest and most beautiful, a calm face, transcendent in dignity. The other two faces were in profile, one gentle and feminine, the other lean and cruel.

"Why are there three faces to this deity?" I inquired of an Indian friend.

"Because the deity, like the human being, has more than one aspect," he replied. "The central face is the face of the Creator. The gentle face is the feminine quality of the Creator's being. The cruel face is his destructive aspect."

"Must there be the feminine?" I asked.

"Assuredly. For the deity also possesses the preserving, guarding function, which is feminine."

"And must he destroy?" I asked again.

"He must destroy if he continues to create, for these are the two opposites in his nature."

The deities of the ancient world were always modeled after the human creature, for Asia understand human nature better than we do. And their deities are always manifold in one as human beings are. To understand that manifold is to understand ourselves—us who were in the beginning created male and female. Together we create, we preserve, two in one and one in two. In us, also, is the destructive element, the desire even to destroy each other, as we do daily when we fail to love completely.

Where does such knowledge begin, so that our young may be educated? It begins in the home, in the treatment the husband and wife, mother and father, accord each to the other. The boy child, in his desire to emulate his father, soon absorbs from him the attitudes of domination over, or consideration for, the wife and mother. What he learns at home he will practice in the community. So, too, the girl child will learn from her parents. If her mother is rebelliously subordinate, or contemptuously superior, to the husband and father, she will never understand her own capacity for love, nor that of the man she will one day marry. For our young enter into marriage almost totally ignorant of each other. They are instructed incorrectly, or at best inadequately, even in physical sex, and they scarcely dream of anything more. Ah, there it is—they do not dream nowadays! They voice their deep discontent in their popular songs, universally sad and lacking in true sexual relation. Out of this hunger and discontent, they seize upon physical sex almost with desperation. A handsome youth put it thus in my presence some time ago. He was speaking of women whom he knew.

"Men seem unable these days to find any common ground with women—except the brief satisfaction of biological need. And that's not enough. It leaves us cold."

"That is the way women feel, too," I said. "They think you want nothing more from them and so that's all they give."

As a result of this sort of desperation there are born each year a quarter of a million unwanted children. For the wanted child is the child born of love and not of desperation. Am I suggesting that we must teach our youths romantic love? Perhaps I am, but for romanticism let me substitute idealism. At least I suggest that we teach respect for human beings, above all for human beings as male and female.

It is not to be expected that every time the male and female come together in the unison of physical sex a child will or should be conceived. Nevertheless, it is true that with each such act a child may be conceived. It is that child who must receive respect, that possible child.

I suggest, therefore, that our education of the young, expressed in factual knowledge and idealism, should include respect for the unborn child, the possible child. The gravest responsibility in life is to bring a child into this world. Under the best of conditions it is a responsibility, for it is an arbitrary act. Not one of us has asked to be born. Two other persons decided upon that. Where society welcomes the child his chances for life are good. Where society does not welcome the child, where he is not wanted, not anticipated, and worst of all, where there is no family to receive him, where even his mother considers him a disaster and his father does not recognize him, where his very existence is a sorrowful secret, then indeed he is to be pitied. He will never receive the respect and love due him unless he finds a substitute family through adoption. More than half the time, however, he will not find that family and he must struggle against the disadvantages of growing up among strangers and alone. For if he does not find father and mother, sisters and brothers, he is alone and among strangers. The primary environment cannot be replaced by employees in a hospital or orphanage, or by paid foster parents.

Yet he enters life bravely. Every boy and girl should learn how bravely a baby enters life. It is no slight ordeal, this matter of birth. None of us understands exactly how the transition is made from the warm liquid world of prenatal life into the totally different atmosphere. Floating in that gentle sea, the baby need not exert his lungs to breathe, nor does he fear a blow or know a touch or suffer hunger. He is altogether protected by his mother. Then comes the moment of birth. Can he survive it? It is the moment of gravest danger for him, more dangerous, perhaps, than he will ever meet again until his death. Will he live? He has only a few seconds, at most a few minutes, in which to decide. As Hippocrates once said, "The occasion is instant." Within the brief space of time his lungs, which he has never used, must begin to function. Until now his mother has supplied him with oxygen and the placental system has disposed, too, of the carbon dioxide in his blood. Now he must do everything for himself. To make it more difficult, his lungs are not clear. They contain fluid, perhaps drawn in before he was born, perhaps created by himself—we do not know. Yet he has to inflate his lungs, expel the fluid and draw in air, or he will die. And all this must be done, I repeat, in seconds or at most in a very few minutes. Meanwhile he is in a surprising, new environment. The comforting darkness he has known until now is gone, and he is surrounded by sharp light. Instead of the warm soft liquid he has hitherto felt on his tender skin, he now feels hard objects of some sort. He is chilled, too, by the new atmosphere. He even feels his own body heavy, which until now has been weightless. Through all this he has only instinct and impulse to guide him.

A weak child cannot cope with the situation. He never draws the first breath, which would catapult him into the new world. He yields and dies. But he is in the minority. The life force is strong and ninety-nine percent of all babies born do fight for their lives. They struggle to draw the first breath, which alone will accommodate them to the new environment, sudden and unexpected, in which they find themselves. It is an act of instinctive courage and it deserves our respect. Therefore, I would, if I were the teacher, educate the young male and female first of all in what it means to be born, to struggle for life, and then to find one's self deprived of family and home. Perhaps, when this lonely individual becomes a reality for them, they will consider their own bodies, their sexual capacities and functions, and perceive the necessity to understand, and to control, and to use wisely the strong and significant power of sex. Am I implying the word *sacred?* It is not a fashionable word, nor one often used in our modern times. It is tarnished by its connection with strict and puritanical religion. Nevertheless, I will use it, for I believe that physical creation is sacred, as art is sacred, and for the same reason. It is creation. And until we imbue our young male and female with recognition of this as a fact, we shall see them desecrate their functions until the sexual act becomes no more than an elimination.

I am not advocating less sex. I am advocating more and better sex, sex that does not shame and degrade an innocent child, sex that brings joy and ecstasy and triumphant pride and, above all, reverence for life.

I do not believe in censorship except by public opinion. Once a group of persons sets itself into a pattern of judging others, untold possibilities arise, all of them dark. But public opinion is something else. It operates individually and the individual can be educated through its legitimate means in any community. Schools and churches, social and service organizations, entertainment and art, all have their part in education. Above all, the home is the central school. What the child learns in the home he remembers all through his life. It shapes his instincts, limits or develops his capacities, and decides whether he will be a free and self-confident human being. Yet the home is created by the man and woman who make it, and the community in turn is the environment which shapes them. Basically, then, the community is responsible for the homes within its area and for the families it shelters. It is in the community that the child is born, and the community cannot ignore or despise any of its children. When a home threatens to disintegrate, the community must see to it that the break is mended. Early perception and diagnosis and treatment must be available.

Every child born out of wedlock is the result of something that is wrong with the home out of which the young male or female has come, and therefore something wrong in the community. The parents were not taught, a good example was not set for them. Love and discipline were not administered in proper form and proportion. Out of their private discontent a man and woman seek each other, and out of discontent a child may be born. For there is no doubt that the sex instinct, always overstimulated by commercialism in our society, provides an outlet for private discontents and inadequacies. Children born out of wedlock are a symptom of failure in the culture. It behooves us, therefore, to study our own society and discover a way of mending the failure by prevention.

I steadfastly recommend education. Let it begin early, as early as the first years in the home through observation of consideration and understanding and love between the parents. Let it be continued by trained teachers, from kindergarten through college. Let it be carried on in the community through mutual respect between men and women, neither denying the other any place or position for which the individual is fitted by nature and inclination. Something like this is taking place in our nation already and the proof is the editorials in some of our newspapers today, approving the possibility of a woman being President of the United States, apropos of Senator Margaret Chase Smith. Without expecting that this will really happen, it is a great advance that even the notion can be entertained without scorn. In its way, it is as significant and civilized an event as the recent declaration by the Catholic Ecumenical Council that Jews are no longer to be held responsible for the death of Jesus of Judea. Let there now be an equally spectacular pronouncement: that no child shall hereafter be called illegitimate, but legitimate by the laws of man as well as of nature, the unwed mother to have status as a mother—and a new era will begin.

Won't this pronouncement result in an increase in the number of children born out of wedlock? Yes, unless education proceeds swiftly enough to teach the young male that he, too, is responsible for the child he begets. Unless both male and female are taught that the child deserves their mutual support in family life, our culture still fails. It is more than a misdemeanor to beget a child without a family. It is an act destructive to our society at the very roots of life.

Certainly the present disorder cannot continue, this hit-and-miss breeding of children who at birth are sent hither and yon in search of families and homes, which half of them never find. It is neither just nor right for a child to be born an orphan. He is born of a father and mother, but he must also be born to a father and mother. In actuality he is so born, and they should not be allowed to evade the responsibility. The child must not be an accident. It is not inevitable that he be born, but once born he is a fact and must be so recognized by his parents and by society.

Until such time, we who work in the field of adoption must continue our efforts. It is incredible, impossible, unbearable, that more than a hundred thousand children are born in our country every year who never find home and family. They are doomed to be orphans, forever deprived of their natural right to a normal childhood. We cannot accept this situation, actual though it is. We must not be content with the merely remedial work we are doing. We must assume leadership in education and change in social attitudes and in the making of new laws until the age comes when the child cannot be born an orphan because, a welcome child, he is born to love and home.

How does a parent love an adopted child? Is it with the same love that he would give, were the child born of his blood and bone and genes? Adoptive parents are advised by agencies to tell the child early that he is adopted, lest someone else tell him rudely or carelessly, thus leaving a wound that cannot be healed. We are also advised, we adoptive parents, to tell the child that he is the especially loved. Ordinary children, we must say, are not always welcome, but the adopted child is always welcome, because he is the chosen one. This is true, but it is not to say that love is always easy in adoption.

In the first place, if we are to begin with the parents, there is a difference between men and women, a general difference with many exceptions. Women, if they love children at all, can love almost any child. The maternal instinct is strong, but over and above and under that must be the ability to love apart from one's self. A woman may have very true maternal instincts as such, but she may not be generous in her gift for love. Thus when a baby is placed in her arms for her own she may or may not feel a rush of innate instincts. If she does it is good, but not enough. For if she is to be a real mother, adoptive or not, but especially if she is adoptive, she must feel the mixed emotions of tenderness and respect—tenderness toward the being for whom she assumes responsibility, respect for the individual whom as yet she does not know. She may not necessarily feel either of these things. Whether she does depends perhaps on her preparation for the event of having a child. She may feel a vague fear, she may even have a seizure of panic, which is not dispelled when her daily life, her placid routine, is disturbed by a demanding baby. She who has considered no one except herself during the hours when she is alone in her house now finds herself never alone. She who slept the whole night through now finds herself waked by an importunate cry, to which she must respond. She may wonder, temporarily, why she ever gave up her placid existence in order to have a child another woman bore. In her remorse for such thoughts and feelings she may find herself miserable.

If so, let her take heart. These are natural feelings, and ephemeral. As the child becomes real to her—a personality delightful though sometimes troublesome, amusing and yet occasionally tiresome—he becomes her own. She forgets that she did not bear him. She believes that she recognizes in him similarities to her own family or to her husband's, and she rejoices when someone says the child looks like one or both of the parents. She compares her child to other children and finds him superior in all important ways. She becomes, in short, a full-fledged mother.

For a man it is usually not so easy. A son is normally his secret desire, the flesh of his flesh, the fruit of his own seed. Though he will not often express it, it is much harder for him to accept the son of another man. The figure he sees is that of a strange man who fathered the child he himself must now call his own. Few men will confess to such feelings but they are there, and they explain the fact that it is much easier for girl babies to find adoptive parents than for boy babies. Do I not know from my own experience? I remember a certain little boy, four months old, his mother Japanese, his father American. The adoptive couple came to see him and the mother fell in love with him at once. The young man who was to be the adoptive father professed the same enthusiasm, ". . . but," he said, "we'll take a few days to think it over."

"Not later than next Tuesday," the mother promised. "I can't wait."

Tuesday came and went. Another week passed. I knew what was happening. I called and the young wife answered, in tears.

"My husband doesn't want the baby boy," she sobbed. "I don't know my own husband. He's always loved children, all children. Every child in the neighborhood comes to our house. It's been the sorrow of our lives that we can't have a child. But he doesn't want the baby. He doesn't know why—just doesn't want him."

"Is there something about this baby?"

"No—he likes the baby, but not for our own."

It is no isolated story. I comforted her as best I could, and hung up the receiver. I told her I was glad her husband was frank, before the baby went to them. The baby found a father eventually, for all men are not the same. There are those who do not think of a son as an extension of themselves, but they are not the majority. Adoption is more than a ceremony. It is a total and final acceptance. It must take deep roots in the conscious and unconscious self before it becomes reality. When it is reality, the bond between parents and child is as deep and, I venture to say, even deeper than the bond of birth. The acceptance can be even more complete, for there are no ghosts of known relatives and inherited genes that might be unfortunate. The adopted child is an entity unto himself and belongs completely to his adoptive parents, as they belong to him.

Yet they must be prepared for a difference between their love for him and his for them. There will come times when he removes himself, when he broods upon his hidden past, when he inquires as to who he really is. It may be true that it is right for him to be told that his are adoptive parents and that he was not born of them, but there are the times when the knowledge is unbear-

able to him, when his whole soul goes in search of himself. Where are the two people who called him into being? Who are they? Must they be forever strangers to him? Is he never to see their faces? As he grows older and into adolescence he finds it hard to forgive them. He tries to forget them, tries to think only of the two who have loved him and cared for him as long as he can remember. He is grateful to them, but the question about himself burns in him. Sometimes he will go in search of his natural parents, nearly always to his own sorrow, for when he finds them he is not welcome. He disrupts their lives. Old secrets are revealed and he finds that what has happened can never be undone. Gazing into the faces of those two, or one, who gave him life by chance, he realizes that they are the strangers and he hastens away from them and back to his own, his adopted, parents.

Should we who adopted allow this search? We cannot forbid it. In my own experience I have always said, "Why not? Let us find the two if we can—or the one, for it is more often one than two. But remember that she had her reasons for giving you up. Should you not respect those reasons? Perhaps you are the secret which she has never told. Consider whether she will be glad to have you come back, full-grown, one whom she cannot escape."

Seldom does the child ever carry out the search when he reflects upon the answers to such questions. For the comfort of adoptive parents, let me say that there is more than relief in this decision of the child not to pursue the search. A new relationship takes place. For the first time, perhaps, the child accepts the adoptive parents fully.

"It is you who have taken care of me always and you are my parents," he will say. And the turmoil ceases, the search is ended and no more questions are asked. The point of all this is, however, that adoptive parents must not allow themselves to be distressed when they go through the turmoil, and they must be patient and answer the questions without reproach. Turmoil and search are part of the adoptive child's growing process. The parents are fortunate if he shares the process with them, if he asks his questions of them instead of hiding them within himself, struggling to find his own answers. They must help the child, too, to realize that it is natural and even right that he should ask who he is, and why he is with them instead of with the other two.

When all questions are answered, or if not answered, accepted as unanswerable, there does remain, however, a permanent wound, which I fear is never entirely healed. It is contained in that old eternal question that strikes at the very root of life.

"How could she give me up?" the child asks.

Ah, how could she? We can never know. How was it that she could not brave the contempt and loneliness and all else that the child born out of wedlock brings to a woman, for the sake of the joy that her child is born? Who can tell? Perhaps it is true that she gave away her child unselfishly for the welfare of the child. Perhaps it was because she did not love the child's father. There is a difference for a woman between having a child by a man she loves and by one she does not love. When she loves the man it is anguish to give up the child who personifies her union with him. One must conclude that most children born out of wedlock are not born of love but by accident. Again I may be wrong. Yet I do not believe that so many girls and women could give up their children otherwise. If love were the source of the passion which produced the child, then those women would defy society—some of them, most of them—and change tradition. But they do not.

I had thought my book finished. But the newspaper carried an item today, a few days before Christmas of this year in which I am writing. I quote:

More than 1,100 boys and girls, each clutching a five-dollar bill, were turned loose in Macy's toy department yesterday to do their own Christmas shopping. The shopping tour for the youngsters, ranging in age from six to eleven, was sponsored by Macy's and the New York City Young Men's Board of Trade. The children came from nineteen metropolitan-area orphanages and welfare homes. A breakfast at the store cafeteria preceded the tour.

So it is still going on! Years ago I first heard of such mass orphan expeditions. I happened one day, a few weeks before Christmas, to turn on the radio for the news. Instead I heard an advertisement from a large department store, which ran something like this:

"Come to our store today and catch the Christmas spirit from the orphans! More than one thousand orphans, each with five dollars, will visit our toy department! Come and see them!"

My first and now continuing response is one of horror and sadness. More than one thousand orphans in a single city, at a single store! Why, why, why? It is the last place I would want to go at any time to see orphans, but especially before Christmas. More than a thousand children without parents or homes, each clutching a five-dollar bill, a composite of tragedy! Why are they still orphans? Yes, this is my first thought. The next is a question. Can it be that I am the only human being who perceives the tragedy and asks the question? Where are the others?

Perhaps one is oversensitive at this season, when love comes welling up out of the heart more than at other times. At this season, for example, I particularly note a sight which wounds me at any time. It is the anger and impatience of too many American mothers with their little children. I cannot bear to see a mother scream and shout at her child. I shiver when I hear the strident voice of a mother threatening her child or see her jerking him along by the arm. Yes, I have heard the excuses of weariness and of having no one to leave the child with, but I know the basic trouble. It is our lack of love for children; it is our lack of respect for the human beings we create. It is not the mother alone who is guilty; it is our whole society, which does not sufficiently treasure the child. When I say treasure, I do not mean the spoiling and lack of discipline, for that too is lack of love and respect. I mean that anger and impatience and physical force reveal lack of love and respect. I feel ashamed when I see such a display. I feel a sense of guilt, since these are my fellow citizens. I love my country and my people. I know our generosities to suffering children in other parts of the world. Why, I ask, do we not love and respect our own?

For these public, almost daily occurrences are not mere incidents. They are symptoms of a deep emotional lack—is it immaturity? I do not know. Why do mothers chafe because they are mothers? Why do fathers pay so little heed to their children? And this whether there is marriage or not? I cannot answer these questions. I only know that the answers are to be found in our lack of love, and in the immaturity which insists upon freedom to do and be what one likes, regardless of others. One does not wish to be independent when one loves; therefore love is lacking, that steadfast love which includes respect for life and all living things, in itself the sign and proof of maturity in an individual and in a people.

The child is the most helpless of creatures. He makes his brave fight at birth, and next to air and food he needs love if he is to continue to live and grow. It is frightening to think of the situation where he is deprived of the security of steadfast love. And who will love him except his parents? He is totally dependent upon them. I contemplate his fear when they are angry with him, the unpredictability of tempers, the swiftness of an unexpected blow, the utter loneliness in which a child lives when he comes to believe himself unloved, and I am struck to the heart. I know, from confidences given to me through the years that many persons grow up in that loneliness and are never able to love anyone because they have not had the experience of love in childhood.

If this can happen in a family, what of those who have no families, those who are rejected at birth by the man and woman who brought them to life? I come back to the point at which I began. Somewhere, somehow, we must consider the nature of love, how to give it, how to receive it. It is the loveless man and woman who threaten our national life and culture. And each was once a loveless child.

About the Author

PEARL S. BUCK was born in West Virginia in 1892 of missionary parents, who went back to China five months later. Her childhood was spent in the historic city of Chinkiang, where she learned to speak Chinese before English, but was taught to write English by her mother. As the child grew older, her mother insisted that she write something every week, and soon these little pieces began to appear in the *Shanghai Mercury*, an English-language newspaper which had a weekly edition for children.

This was the start of a brilliant literary career, although it was not until 1922 that Miss Buck's first article appeared in an American magazine, the *Atlantic Monthly*. Her first novel was *East Wind: West Wind*, which grew out of a story published in *Asia Magazine*. It became successful in its own right; before *The Good Earth* was published ten months later, in 1932, *East Wind: West Wind* was in its third printing.

The Good Earth stood on the American list of best sellers for twenty-one months and won the Pulitzer Prize for that year. It was translated into more than thirty languages, including the Chinese in which there are several different versions. In November, 1935, the author was awarded the Howells Medal for *The Good Earth* as "the most distinguished work of American fiction" published in the previous five years. In 1936 she was elected a member of the National Institute of Arts and Letters. In 1938 she received the Nobel Prize for literature, the first American woman to be so honored.

All of her life Miss Buck has been interested in the problems of children—retarded, orphaned, of mixed racial lines. She herself has raised nine adopted children in addition to her own child. Her most recent activities, other than her writing, have been the establishment in 1949 of Welcome House, Inc., an adoption agency which finds permanent homes and parents for children of mixed Asian-American heritage, and the Pearl S. Buck Foundation, designed for the welfare and education of these children born of American fathers and Asian mothers, who must remain in the countries where they are born.